TOWARD
A JEWISH THEOLOGY
OF LIBERATION

TOWARD
A JEWISH THEOLOGY
OF LIBERATION

The Uprising and the Future

Marc H. Ellis

ORBIS BOOKS

Maryknoll, New York 10545

296.3
E47I
1987

The Catholic Foreign Mission Society of America (Maryknoll) recruits and trains people for overseas missionary service. Through Orbis Books Maryknoll aims to foster the international dialogue that is essential to mission. The books published, however, reflect the opinions of their authors and are not meant to represent the official position of the society.

ISBN 0-88344-434-8
ISBN 0-88344-422-4 (pbk.)

To my father and mother
Herbert Moore Ellis
and
June Goldwin Ellis

who first taught me the meaning
of Jewish ethics and liberation

and
to my son
Aaron Moore Ellis

May he be a blessing to the household
of Israel

Blessed is the match that is consumed
in kindling flame.
Blessed is the flame that burns
in the secret fastness of the heart.
Blessed is the heart with strength to stop
its beating for honor's sake.
Blessed is the match that is consumed
in kindling flame.

Hannah Senesch

Stop the beatings, stop the breaking of bones, stop the late-night raids on people's homes, stop the use of food as a weapon of war, stop pretending that you can respond to an entire people's agony with guns and blows and power. Publicly acknowledge that the Palestinians have the same right to national self-determination that we Jews have and negotiate a solution with representatives of the Palestinians!

Michael Lerner

Contents

Preface to the Second Edition

Writing this preface provokes mixed emotions. On the one hand, I am pleased, as is any author, that my book has found an audience, that my ideas have elicited a response and often a sense of solidarity. On the other hand, I am saddened that the realities which I analyze in this book continue and in some ways have worsened. The Palestinian uprising has brought to the attention of the world and, in a profound sense, to the attention of the Jewish people, the suffering and hope of the Palestinian people. It has forced all of us, myself included, to deepen our reflection and encourage action on behalf of peace with justice in the Middle East. Hence, this edition carries as a final chapter an afterword which calls for a theological conversion of the Jewish people toward those whom we often see as the enemy. How many people will be beaten, tortured, or murdered, how many imprisoned or deported, before we understand that solidarity is the way toward a future worth bequeathing to our children? My hope is that this edition will bring us one step closer to the ethical witness which lies at the heart of what it means to be Jewish.

Preface to the First Edition

Like any study, this book is informed and limited by the particular experience and background of its author. A practicing Jew, I am a student of contemporary religious thought rather than a trained Jewish theologian. This book, therefore, does not attempt to expound an academic Jewish theology but rather to surface dialectics, issues, and possibilities that might give birth to a Jewish theology of liberation. Depending on one's perspective, my study of and work with progressive Roman Catholic groups and institutions such as the Catholic Worker movement and the Maryknoll Fathers and Brothers may evoke fear or wonder. These affiliations, however, rather than impeding my faith, have yielded a perspective that has renewed my Jewish outlook and commitment. Like many other Jewish and Christian believers, I affirm the continuity of the Judeo-Christian tradition. I regard Christianity, or perhaps more appropriately, contemporary followers of Jesus, as issuing from the Jewish community and following a stream of ideas, beliefs, and values that are similar and yet distinct from those of the contemporary Jewish people. I view the separation of faith communities as tragic, for it is a source of much pain and confusion. The Jewish prayers said each morning that thank God for making one a Jew and calling one to be free, represent for me a hope that my faith can lead to authentic solidarity with all those who struggle for human dignity and justice.

Acknowledgments

I wish to express my appreciation to Stephen Scharper, Eve Drogin, Robert Gormley, and the staff of Orbis Books for their encouragement and help in editing and producing this book. I am especially indebted to the late Philip Scharper, who first expressed interest in a book on a Jewish theology of liberation. I am also indebted to *Theology in the Americas,* which published my first article on the subject. Rosalida Ramirez and Martha Robson were especially helpful in this regard. I am grateful to Temple Sinai in Toronto, Canada, the Ecumenical Institute at Tantur, Jerusalem, the Development Studies Program in Dublin, Ireland, and DEI in Costa Rica, for encouraging me to explore these theological themes in diverse settings. Temple Israel of Northern Westchester in Croton-on-Hudson, New York, and especially Rabbi Michael Robinson, have provided a place of worship and social commitment that has deeply enriched my life. My students in the Institute for Justice and Peace at the Maryknoll School of Theology first listened to these ideas and saw me wrestle with them in the more difficult times. That the Maryknoll Society has provided a place for a Jew to teach, study, write, and travel is for me a sign of a future we can only now imagine. Their struggle to be faithful in Latin America, Africa, and Asia has deeply influenced my own understanding of fidelity, and to them I will be eternally grateful. To Ann McDonald, the first and final editor of this book, a person who has lived with these ideas during the weekdays and often on *Shabbat,* I can only say "thank you." Georgene Viggiano has been a cheerful typist and a friend, as have Clara Araujo and Geri DiLauro. Finally, my thanks go to my "teachers," Paul Picard, Lawrence Cunningham, David Taylor, Rosemary Ruether, Pablo Richard, William Miller, Matthew Lamb, Paul Hansen, James Cone, Otto Maduro, and Richard Rubenstein. Their committed scholarship continues to provide a foundation for a just and peaceful way of life.

Introduction

The history of the Jewish people is filled with anguish and struggle. More often than not, the defining motif of Jewish life has been exile, forced wandering, and lament. And yet, through this travail the Jewish community has bequeathed much to the world: a developed monotheism, a prophetic social critique, an awareness of God's presence in history, and the foundation of two other world religions, Christianity and Islam.

As important as these contributions are for the Jewish community, of which I am a part, the paradigm of liberation that forms the heart of the Jewish experience, the dynamic of bondage confronted by the call to freedom, has been appropriated also by struggling peoples throughout the ages. The songs of African slaves in nineteenth-century America calling on God for freedom echo the lamentations of the Jews in Egypt. The Exodus tradition, articulated in the writings of Latin American liberation theologians, again emerges within the struggle of Latin Americans for justice.

To cite these contributions of the Jewish people is to pose a fundamental contradiction of world history, one posed often but answered only weakly. Why is it that a people that has contributed so much to the world has received such scornful treatment in return? Why is it that Jews today are considered not as principal contributors to Western religious and intellectual heritage, but only as victims and survivors? And why is it that in these allegedly enlightened times a people born of suffering is doubted and dismissed, as if the world should have no concern for a people's long and difficult history? And finally, why is the quest for a just and safe existence, so prized by the secular and religious left, denied to a small and suffering people just emerging from the death camps of Nazi Germany? Have not the Jewish people been ostracized, even condemned, for their difficult passage to empowerment in the State

1

of Israel? Indeed, to a progressive Jew who has tried to understand the rebirth of a prophetic Christianity and affirm the humanist community of our day, comprised of nonreligious persons who embrace the values of dignity and justice, these contradictions are haunting.

The paradox of achievement and suffering is only part of Jewish history. To be sure, the overwhelming motif of wandering and exile flows from a fidelity to covenantal truths and values, an innocence often rewarded with brutality. On the other hand, the Jewish community's struggle to be faithful to those values has been shadowed by the reality of betrayal, for in advance of our own interests we have been slave merchants and masters, supported corrupt kings and governments, and even at times oppressed one another.

Today, in Israel and in the Jewish community in North America, policies and alliances increasingly resemble those historically used to oppress our own people. On the Israeli side one need only mention the recently-concluded occupation of Lebanon and the continuing subjugation of West Bank and Gaza Palestinians; just as horrific are the relations Israel maintains with South Africa and Israel's military assistance to the murderous governments of El Salvador and Guatemala. In North America efforts continue to establish Israel as a U.S. outpost by building up its military. Relations between American Jewry and the poor and oppressed of North America remain strained, and the ambivalent courtship of Israel by fundamentalist Christians continues. It is not too much to say that these developments threaten the very existence of the Jewish people. A crossroads appears that calls us to fidelity to our values though it may yet tempt us to betrayal of those values.

The choice between fidelity and betrayal arises from the history of our people, guided as they are by the image of "enslaved ancestors," as Walter Benjamin once wrote. To be faithful to our ancestors, particularly those who have struggled, suffered and died in the Holocaust, is to be attentive to their cries, which must guide us. But fidelity to our own values and history is intimately connected to the struggles for liberation of others; the brokenness of our past is betrayed, our political empowerment made suspect, when others become our victims.

Poised between Holocaust and political empowerment, we in the Jewish community find it increasingly difficult to articulate a witness consonant with our past. The thunderings of expansionist Israelis and of neoconservative North American Jews witness to the haunting possibility of a Judaism lost. Other Jews, often less articulate and removed from centers of power, are caught within this dialectic, fearing to speak yet distinctly uncomfortable with the direction our community is taking. Still others, intellectuals and activists within Israel and North America, actively oppose the paths already chosen by the institutional representatives of the Jewish community. Yet how, in our post-Holocaust world, do we articulate these feelings and opposition? And who is to name betrayal and fidelity?

Although there is no corner on truth here and the risks for the Jewish community are great, the discussion cannot continue to be censored. Every community has patterns of fidelity and betrayal, points of paralysis and breakthrough, and the Jewish community is no exception. Patterns move us beyond the incidental and isolated example to movements toward and away from the central ideals of the community, ideals forged in historical struggle and affirmation. In history final resolutions are impossible. What thus becomes important is the direction in which a community moves.

However, at certain times in history the community reaches a crossroads it cannot seem to articulate or acknowledge. This is the point of paralysis where rational thought, even the wisdom of one's tradition, seems to falter. The community drifts; the rhetoric drones on; judgment becomes clouded. Paralysis is less an evil than an indicator that the comunity needs to review its inner dynamic and its relations with other communities. Questions are posed. Does our present situation, if pursued, lead us to justice and renewal, or to emptiness and oppression? Are our discussions addressing the values and witness we are called to live, or are they covering over a hope we refuse to face because of its difficulty? Some historical situations might demand accentuation of particular values and the de-emphasis of others, and there are times no doubt when the community is simply bereft of values, exhausted, as it were, by history's travails. Are we willing to admit this state so we can begin the process of renewal?

If we come to understand points of paralysis, the possibility of breakthrough increases. Of course, the problem is that patterns of fidelity and betrayal occur in the mix of history, and the lessons of history are often as ambivalent as they are terrifying. Proponents and opponents, prophets and villains appear at every turn, defined by angles of vision and experience that depend on various propensities and points of view. What to one faction is a breakthrough may be to the other an apocalypse. This is the dilemma in which the Jewish people of North America and the State of Israel—the two most articulate and politically powerful Jewish communities—presently find themselves.

To say that the questions raised by this situation are controversial is an understatement. The deep hurt of the Jewish people, their historical and contemporary sense of isolation, their feeling of being adrift in a hostile world: these are intensely subjective memories and emotions which spring from our history. To speak publicly on issues of the Holocaust and Israel in a critical manner is to court suspicion and raise the spectre of treason. The result may be excommunication from the Jewish community, or worse, the accusation that one is supporting the climate for another holocaust. But the difficult questions remain, and the movement of our lives and community, toward fidelity or betrayal, lies before us.

This book is one attempt to address the crisis that confronts us. Chapter One begins with the Holocaust and the pain and vision that issue from it. Theology that emerges from the Holocaust is crucial, for to a large extent it responds to a consensus within the Jewish community. Controversial in its origins, Holocaust theology now is accepted as the way to the future.

A central theme of Chapter Two is political empowerment and the theological rationale that undergirds it. At the same time, certain persons are trying to assess the cost of this empowerment, something to which Holocaust theologians initially gave little thought. We find a debate over the relationship of political empowerment and ethical concern—a debate that is crucial for the future of the Jewish community.

The concrete expression and limitations of ethical concern is the subject of Chapter Three. The findings are ambiguous, because the depth of ethical commitment is astounding while the acceptance of movements of renewal in the larger community is less than encouraging. Although the theology of empowerment leaves little room for prophetic challenge, such a prophetic voice continues to be heard in an exilic way.

Chapter Four is an excursion outside the Jewish community to Christian liberation movements that, paradoxically, despite Christianity's long history of abuse and oppression of the Jewish people, carry forth the tradition of the Exodus, of the prophets and the refusal of idolatry that we bequeathed to the world. The question posed here is whether we will show solidarity with those struggling for justice and, in so doing, recover our own history and witness. The Holocaust is again discussed, now in the broader framework of other suffering peoples, and the issue of Jewish contribution to suffering in North America and Israel is brought to the fore. Can we bond with those who are suffering today if we do not look honestly at the history we are creating? To enter into solidarity with suffering peoples, however, we need to look again at our own history, especially in relation to the Holocaust and the State of Israel.

Chapter Five suggests that one way of doing this is to allow the journeys and visions of dissenting Jews to reemerge. Of the many we could choose, we discuss Etty Hillesum and Martin Buber because they address the difficult question of God's presence in an age of holocaust and the essential link between the Jewish return to Palestine and the Palestinian people. In order to move beyond the unexamined assumptions and the inflexibility of certain positions, the path untaken forces us to reexamine the "truths" we affirm. Could it be that the majority Jewish understanding of God and the State of Israel, reinforced with emotion and argument, covers over another perspective on what it means to be Jewish?

From the preceding discussion the themes of contemporary Jewish life that have surfaced are brought together in Chapter Six in a new framework. The dialectic of the Holocaust and political empowerment, confronted by renewal and solidarity as the way to recover our history and witness, is the path of liberation. Liberation cannot avoid the difficult questions, and this chapter seeks to move beyond Holocaust theology to a Jewish theology of liberation. Such a theology represents a willingness to enter the danger zones of contemporary Jewish life and examine the liberal rhetoric and activity that protect our recently acquired affluence and power. The aim is to help create, in concert with others, an atmosphere in which the deepest parts of our tradition can speak in the language of fidelity.

CHAPTER 1

A Shattered Witness

One cannot understand the Jewish community today without a sense of its past, for it was born in struggle and hope. Geographically, the beginnings of the Jewish community obviously lie in ancient Egypt, as is recalled in the Hebrew Scriptures. The experience of slavery and liberation, though, repeated time and again in Jewish history, marks the last two thousand years as a time of movement in exile rather than of liberation. To repeatedly withstand intense communal suffering is necessarily to take seriously both the community's history and its promise of freedom. Interpretation of events becomes crucial, even consuming: at the heart of Jewish life is the dialectic of slavery and liberation, a paradox to be thought through in each generation.[1]

For contemporary Jews, the overwhelming experience of suffering is the Jewish Holocaust, the death of six million Jews and the attempted annihilation of our entire people. Interpretation of the event is omnipresent, though insights are diverse and often controversial. One might say that the Holocaust is the formative event for the Jewish community of today and provides the framework from which the struggle to be faithful to our values takes shape.

To delve into the Holocaust world is to be surrounded with the agony of a people on the threshold of annihilation. Survivors' accounts, histories, even the documentary *Shoah,* which includes testimonies of both survivors and perpetrators of the Holocaust, all point to the same incredible reality: a Kingdom of Death built by the Nazis to consume an ancient people—quite simply, to eliminate

7

all Jews from the face of the earth. Within the Holocaust Kingdom, Jews from all over the world struggled to understand, survive and even to resist actively the Nazi goal of annihilation. Existing on the other side of history in ghettos, concentration camps, and death camps, these Jewish voices provide the memories and context for contemporary Jewish life.

The witnesses are diverse and poignant, and to hear their voices is difficult; they sound like discordant notes rather than a melody. The struggle to live is challenged by the desire to die; resistance is countered by helplessness. The sense of isolation and abandonment is omnipresent. They are witnesses from another world.

The desire to die is perhaps the most difficult for us to affirm. The situation, however, calls us to an understanding. A Jewish mother of Eastern Europe relates her story of survival as a prayer for death. She and others had been herded onto a field, sprayed with machine-gun fire, and buried in a pit with those dead and dying.

> And yet with my last strength I came up on the top of the grave, and when I did, I did not know the place, so many bodies were lying all over, dead people; I wanted to see the end of this stretch of dead bodies but I could not. It was impossible. They were lying all over, all dying; suffering, not all of them dead, but in their last sufferings; naked; shot, but not dead. . . . I was searching among the dead for my little girl, and I cried for her—Merkele was her name—"Merkele!" There were children crying "Mother," "Father"—but they were all smeared with blood and one could not recognize the children. I cried for my daughter. I was praying for death to come. I was praying for the grave to be opened and to swallow me alive. Blood was spurting from the grave in many places, like a well of water, and whenever I pass a spring now, I remember the blood which spurted from the ground, from that grave. I dug with my fingernails, but the grave would not open. I did not have enough strength. I cried out to my mother, to my father, "Why did they not kill me? What was my sin? I have no one to go to." I saw them all being killed. Why was I spared? Why was I not killed?[2]

In the face of evil, helplessness was often the order of the day. Women who became pregnant in the camps were sent to their death as punishment for the ultimate affirmation of life: conceiving new life. And women who somehow concealed their pregnancy and gave birth found their babies drowned by Nazi guards before their eyes. Mothers were often asked by the authorities to select which of their children would be spared and which would be sent to their death. Thus the givers of life were forced to become accomplices in the murder of their own children.

These horror stories are hardly random tales. The death of Jews was logically and legally planned. Mass death was systematic; sporadic murder was in fact discouraged. The extermination of the Jews came about through a complex series of acts that started by defining who was a Jew. Since the Nazis defined Jews as a racial type rather than as a people with professed beliefs, categorization did not come easily. Lineage was traced, the mixture of other "races" through intermarriage ascertained and judged. Finally a decision was rendered; once a person was defined as a Jew, personal property and rights of citizenship were withdrawn; thus Jews were instantaneously rendered poor and stateless. At the outset this required laws and decrees, transfers of property and employment, and a plan to relocate those who were now by definition and ability outside of German society. From that point the outcome was predictable, even logical, within the Nazi framework: elimination. This plan necessitated an intricate system of transportation and receiving facilities for the vast numbers of those now dislocated. Indeed, the elimination of the Jews had become a system requiring the cooperation of every sector of German society. As Richard Rubenstein writes, "The bureaucrats drew up the definitions and decrees; the Churches gave evidence of Aryan descent; the postal authorities carried the messages of definition, expropriation, denationalization and deportation; business corporations dismissed their Jewish employees and took over 'Aryanized' properties; the railroads carried the victims to their place of execution."[3]

Through all of this suffering, the feeling of isolation and abandonment reigns. The Western world's failure to accept Jewish refugees and to develop a policy of Jewish rescue, including the refusal to destroy the death camps so as to cripple the capability of the Nazis to continue their slaughter, has now been amply documented. Even the question of whether the Western powers and the populace at large knew of the atrocities has been investigated and answered affirmatively. Canada, which had been advertising for settlers for over a hundred years, illustrates the Western policy. A reporter went to a government official and asked if the doors of the country were going to be opened to Jewish refugees. The official responded that Canada did not want too many Jews. The reporter then asked, "How many is too many?" The response: "None is too many."[4]

But well before the retrospective studies were concluded, the victims already understood their abandonment. As Alexander Donat, a survivor of Treblinka, records:

> In vain we looked at that cloudless September sky for some sign of God's wrath. The heavens were silent. In vain we waited to hear from the lips of the great ones of the world, the champions of light and justice, the Roosevelts, the Churchills, the Stalins, the words of thunder, the threat of massive retaliation that might have halted the executioner's axe. In vain we implored help from our Polish brothers with whom we had shared good and bad fortune alike for seven centuries, but they were utterly unmoved in our hour of anguish. They did not show even normal human compassion at our ordeal, let alone demonstrate Christian charity. They did not even let political good sense guide them; for after all we were objectively allies in a struggle against a common enemy. While we bled and died, their attitude was at best indifference, and all too often friendly neutrality to the Germans. Let the Germans do this dirty work for us.[5]

This is the legacy left after the end of World War II. The event is so overwhelming that it took nearly two decades to name it the Holocaust. Its meaning remains even more problematic, and Jewish theologians are left with this difficult task. Over the years essentially four basic positions on the meaning of the event have emerged, represented by four major Jewish thinkers: Elie Wiesel, writer and survivor of the Holocaust; Richard Rubenstein, a professor of religious studies at Florida State University; Emil Fackenheim, formerly a professor of philosophy at the University of

Toronto; and Irving Greenberg, a rabbi and Director of the National Jewish Center for Learning and Leadership in New York City. One point at least is agreed upon: fidelity to the Jewish people in the present lies in grappling with this experience of destruction and death.

ELIE WIESEL

Elie Wiesel's fundamental struggle to be faithful is found in the recounting of the story itself. Through fiction, essays, and public talks Wiesel has spent a lifetime trying to put into words the indescribable and to articulate the unimaginable as an expression of his fidelity to the experience of the victims.

All those uprooted communities, ravaged and dissolved in smoke; all those trains that criss-crossed the nocturnal Polish landscapes; all those men, all those women, stripped of their language, their names, their faces, compelled to live and die according to the laws of the enemy, in anonymity and darkness. All those kingdoms of barbed wire where everyone looked alike and all words carried the same weight. Day followed day and hour followed hour, while thoughts, numb and bleak, groped their way among the corpses, through the mire and the blood.

And the adolescent in me, yearning for faith, questioned: Where was God in all this? Was this another test, one more? Or a punishment? And if so, for what sins? What crimes were being punished? Was there a misdeed that deserved so many mass graves? Would it ever again be possible to speak of justice, of truth, of divine charity, after the murder of one million Jewish children?

I did not understand, I was afraid to understand. Was this the end of the Jewish people, or the end perhaps of the human adventure? Surely it was the end of an era, the end of a world. That I knew, that was all I knew.[6]

From the first, he knew that, as a survivor, he was called to witness. What eluded him was how to answer that call.

> I knew that the role of the survivor was to testify. Only I did not know how. I lacked experience, I lacked a framework. I mistrusted the tools, the procedures. Should one say it all or hold it all back? Should one shout or whisper? Place the emphasis on those who were gone or on their heirs? How does one describe the indescribable? How does one use restraint in recreating the fall of mankind and the eclipse of the gods? And then, how can one be sure that the words, once uttered, will not betray, distort the message they bear? So heavy was my anguish that I made a vow not to speak, not to touch upon the essential for at least ten years. Long enough to see clearly. Long enough to learn to listen to the voices crying inside my own. Long enough to regain possession of my memory. Long enough to unite the language of man with the silence of the dead.[7]

Yet Wiesel's task is to find a voice for the voiceless and to keep alive a memory that is always on the verge of extinction. The task of remembrance is, in a sense, more important than an answer to the meaning of suffering, because for many there is no answer.

For Wiesel, the question of belief undergoes a traumatic reversal in the death camps. Coming from a religious home, Wiesel as a young boy experiences the shattering of his faith soon after arriving at Auschwitz.

> Never shall I forget that night, the first night in camp, which has turned my life into one long night, seven times cursed and seven times sealed. Never shall I forget that smoke. Never shall I forget the little faces of the children, whose bodies I saw turned into wreaths of smoke beneath a silent blue sky.
>
> Never shall I forget those flames which consumed my faith forever.
>
> Never shall I forget that nocturnal silence which deprived me for all eternity of the desire to live. Never shall I forget those moments which murdered my God and my soul and turned my dreams to dust. Never shall I forget these things, even if I am condemned to live as long as God Himself. Never.[8]

From that moment on Wiesel struggles with two apparently irreconcilable realities—the reality of God and the reality of Auschwitz.
As Robert McAfee Brown comments in his *Elie Wiesel: Messenger
to All Humanity,* "Either seems able to cancel out the other, and yet
neither will disappear. Either in isolation could be managed—
Auschwitz and no God or God and no Auschwitz. But Auschwitz
and God, God *and* Auschwitz?" At Rosh Hashanah, the Jewish
new year, Wiesel records his reaction when ten thousand inmates
repeat the Jewish prayer "Blessed be the Name of the Eternal."

> Why, but why should I bless Him? In every fiber I rebelled.
> Because He had had thousands of children burned in His
> pits? Because He kept six crematories working night and day,
> on Sundays and feast days? Because in His great might He
> had created Auschwitz, Birkenau, Buna, and so many factor-
> ies of death? How could I say to Him: "Blessed art Thou,
> Eternal, Master of the Universe, Who chose us from among
> the races to be tortured day and night, to see our fathers, our
> mothers, our brothers, end in the crematory? Praised be Thy
> Holy Name, Thou Who hast chosen us to be butchered on
> Thine altar"?[9]

And later at the hanging of three inmates, one of them a child,
someone behind Wiesel asks, "Where is God? Where is He?" As
the chairs are toppled and the three victims swing with the ropes
around their necks, the prisoners are marched by at close range.

> The two adults were no longer alive. Their tongues hung
> swollen, blue-tinged. But the third rope was still moving;
> being so light, the child was still alive. . . .
>
> For more than half an hour he stayed there, struggling
> between life and death, dying a slow agony under our eyes.
> And we had to look him full in the face. He was still alive
> when I passed in front of him. His tongue was still red, his
> eyes not yet glazed.
>
> Behind me, I heard the same man asking: "Where is God
> now?"
>
> And I heard a voice within me answer him: "Where is He?
> Here He is—He is hanging here on this gallows. . . ."[10]

Through the experience of the death camps an innocence that cannot be recovered is lost. The world has changed, and so has faith. Prayer is replaced by memory: memory is a prayer articulated in solemn silence. For those who remain within the "fiery world of holocaust," the fires of the crematorium still smolder; the skeletons remain as they were, piled high and naked. Wiesel's mission is simply put: "Anyone who does not actively engage in remembering is an accomplice of the enemy. Conversely, whoever opposes the enemy must take the side of his victims and communicate their tales, tales of solitude and despair, tales of silence and defiance."[11]

The reliability of remembrance can hardly be assumed, because so much has been stripped away. Testimony itself becomes naked, and the tradition with its layers of symbol and word no longer is available. Wiesel uses a Hassidic tale to describe the situation.

When the great Rabbi Israel Baal Shem-Tov saw misfortune threatening the Jews it was his custom to go into a certain part of the forest to meditate. There he would a light a fire, say a special prayer and the miracle would be accomplished and the misfortune averted.

Later, when his disciple, the celebrated Magid of Mezeritch, had occasion, for the same reason, to intercede with heaven, he would go to the same place in the forest and say, "Master of the Universe, listen! I do not know how to light the fire, but I am still able to say the prayer," and again the miracle would be accomplished.

Still later, Rabbi Moseh-Leib of Sasov, in order to save his people once more, would go into the forest and say: "I do not know how to light the fire, I do not know the prayer, but I know the place and this must be sufficient." It was sufficient and the miracle was accomplished.

Then it fell to Rabbi Israel of Rizhyn to overcome misfortune. Sitting in his armchair, his head in his hands, he spoke to God: "I am unable to light the fire and I do not know the prayer; I cannot even find the place in the forest. All I can do is to tell the story, and this must be sufficient."

And it was sufficient.[12]

RICHARD RUBENSTEIN

For Richard Rubenstein the stories of the dead coalesce in a different way. The challenge of Auschwitz is not simply to remember, but to investigate its meaning in its religious and historical dimensions. The religious dimension is complex, relating to a belief in a God of history, to the tradition within which Jews place themselves, and to the leadership of the Jewish community. Rubenstein sees all three aspects as contributing to the death of six million, and each is thus negated in the Holocaust event. The omnipotent, benevolent God of history is shown to be a farce in the face of systematic death of the innocent. God, indeed, is a culpable figure, for belief in their chosenness (a belief inculcated by God) supported Jewish acquiescence in the events around them, sure as they were that they would be preserved amid the destruction. The tradition that posits suffering as an integral part of this special relationship with God also is called to accountability, for it did not provide the foundation for clarity of thought or for armed resistance to human evil. Stressing wandering and suffering as an affirmation of Jewishness, the tradition encouraged passivity in the face of annihilation. At the same time, some Jewish leaders embodied a belief in God and compliance with those authorities who sought annihilation of all Jews. Jewish councils in Europe presided over the ghettos, provided all basic services to the people (including the policing of the ghetto), and fulfilled Nazi orders, even to the point of organizing the evacuation of Jews to the death camps.[13]

Jewish compliance with such authorities is critical to Rubenstein's understanding of the failure of Jewish tradition in the face of annihilation, a compliance intimately connected with Jewish history. According to Rubenstein, the last time the Jews had taken up arms against an enemy was during the Judeo-Roman Wars of 66–70 and 131–35 of the Common Era. On both occasions, they fought valiantly and lost disastrously. Those who counseled surrender became the religious and political leaders of the Jewish people. As Rubenstein states, "The religious leaders of the European diaspora for almost two thousand years were the spiritual heirs of the Pharisees and rabbis who rose to political and religious dominance only after they had been selected by the Romans as their 'loyal and nonseditious agents.' " Thus, diaspora Judaism began in military defeat and survived by developing a culture of surrender and submission.[14]

The heir of that tradition, rabbinic Judaism, helped to shape and condition Jewish responses for two thousand years. Despite secularization and emancipation, the Jewish community continued to "respond to overlords as had those who had surrendered to the Romans." Instead of armed resistance, they sought to avert hostile action by bribery, petitions for mercy, appeal to ethical sentiments, or flight. In fact, the organized Jewish community was a major factor in preventing effective resistance. "Wherever the extermination process was put into effect, the Germans utilized the existing leadership and organization of the Jewish community to assist them. It was not necessary to find traitors or collaborators to do their work. The compliance reaction was automatic." There was some sporadic resistance to the Germans, the most spectacular being the 1943 Warsaw Ghetto uprising, but this was the exception. The overwhelming majority of Jews did not resist. "They had been conditioned by their religious culture to submit and endure. There was no resort to even token violence when the Nazis forced Jews to dig mass graves, strip, climb into the graves, lie down over the layer of corpses already murdered and await the final coup de grace." This submission was the final chapter in the history of a cultural and psychological transformation begun by the rabbis and Pharisees almost two thousand years earlier.[15]

For Rubenstein, those three factors—the failure of God, Jewish tradition, and Jewish leadership—signal the end of Jewish life as we know it. To persevere in pre-Holocaust patterns of Jewish life is to indulge a fantasy that portends a repetition of the Holocaust event. Yet this failure moves beyond the Jewish community; the Jewish Holocaust represents the severing of the relationship between God and person, God and community, God and culture. The lesson of the Holocaust is that humanity is alone and that there is no meaning in life outside of human solidarity.

The Jewish Holocaust also throws into question the possibility of human solidarity, for it introduces systematic mass death as a permanent possibility of the increasingly powerful state. Secular society is characterized by a bureaucratic rationality that renders entire populations superfluous in a time when population increases exponentially. In other words, just as more persons come into the world, their social and political importance is diminished—a situation that often leads to mass executions. For Rubenstein, a moral and political landmark in the history of Western civilization was achieved by the Nazis in World War II: the systematic, bureaucratically administered extermination of millions of citizens or subject peoples is now one of the capacities and temptations of government. In effect, Auschwitz has enlarged our conception of the state's capacity to do violence. "A barrier has been overcome in what for millennia had been regarded as the permissible limits of political action. The Nazi period serves as a warning of what we can all too easily become were we faced with a political or an economic crisis of overwhelming proportions. The public may be fascinated by the Nazis; hopefully, it is also warned by them."[16]

Thus the secular world born of the death of religious belief promises little more, or perhaps even less, to human flourishing and advance. In sum, one sees a tragic impasse: the religious world collapses of its own inadequacy, and the modern world devours its own children.[17]

Rubenstein's understanding thus differs from Wiesel's in significant ways. Wiesel's overall sensibility is in story: the recounting of the horror and a willingness to remain in the tension of belief, though silent and unnamed. The way to prevent another holocaust is to preserve the memory of the first. For Rubenstein, the tension of belief is broken and holocaust continues unabated. The need now is to create a political sensibility within the Jewish community and outside of it that responds to the social, economic, and political crises of modern life. If Wiesel's fidelity is found in remembering suffering, Rubenstein's is defined by his refusal to accept indiscriminate evil as an attribute of divinity and by his emphasis on the necessity of human solidarity in a desacralized world.[18]

EMIL FACKENHEIM

The thought of Emil Fackenheim finds a middle ground between Wiesel and Rubenstein. For Fackenheim, the Holocaust is a challenge to both faith and secularism as found in the Jewish context. The midrashic framework of interpretation, which sees present experience as continuous with the past and therefore counterposes the two to lend depth to interpretation and mystery, breaks down in the cataclysmic event of the Holocaust. Root experiences, such as the Exodus, are challenged and overturned as clarity of faith is diminished. However, the secular option is also challenged, because the secular Jew was also singled out for annihilation. Even in claiming status as a born Jew, the secularist gives testimony to the survival of the Jewish people. "For a Jew today merely to affirm his Jewish existence is to accept his singled-out condition; it is to oppose the demons of Auschwitz: and it is to oppose them in the only way in which they can be opposed—with an absolute opposition. Moreover, it is to stake on that absolute opposition nothing less than his life and the lives of his children and the lives of his children's children."[19]

After Auschwitz, the Jew who claims affiliation with the Jewish people is a witness to endurance, because Jewish survival is a dangerous and holy duty. In another sense, this identification as Jew after the Holocaust offers humanity survival and testimony in an age jeopardized by nuclear confrontation. Thus Fackenheim rules out two possibilities as authentic responses to the Holocaust: abandoning Jewish identification with poor and persecuted peoples, and using identification with the world to flee from Jewish destiny. Ultimately, in the event that one must choose between two suffering peoples, the Jew must identify with the Jewish people. This identification is the essence of the comanding voice of Auschwitz.

Jews are forbidden to hand Hitler posthumous victories. They are commanded to survive as Jews, lest the Jewish people perish. They are commanded to remember the victims of Auschwitz lest their memory perish. They are forbidden to despair of man and his world, and to escape into either cynicism or otherworldliness, lest they cooperate in delivering the world over to the forces of Auschwitz. Finally, they are forbidden to despair of the God of Israel, lest Judaism perish.[20]

The commanding voice of Auschwitz is heard today because the command to survive was heard within Auschwitz. The Nazi logic of destruction was irresistible, and yet for Fackenheim it was resisted. This Nazi logic is a *novum* in human history, the "source of an unprecedented, abiding horror." But resistance to it on the part of the most radically exposed is also a *novum* in history, and it is the "source of an unprecedented, abiding wonder." For Fackenheim, to hear and obey the commanding voice of Auschwitz is a possibility today because the hearing and obeying was a reality in the death camps. Fackenheim cites Pelagia Lewinska, a survivor of the Holocaust, as illustrating this commanding voice.

> At the outset the living places, the ditches, the mud, the piles of excrement behind the blocks, had appalled me with their horrible filth. . . . And then I saw the light! I saw that it was not a question of disorder or lack of organization but that, on the contrary, a very thoroughly considered conscious idea was in the back of the camp's existence. They had condemned us to die in our own filth, to drown in mud, in our own excrement. They wished to abase us, to destroy our human dignity, to efface every vestige of humanity. . . . From the instant when I grasped the motivating principle. . . it was as if I had been awakened from a dream. . . . I felt under orders to live. . . . And if I did die in Auschwitz, it would be as a human being. I would hold on to my dignity.[21]

Fackenheim's fidelity to the experience of Holocaust places him with neither Wiesel nor Rubenstein, yet close in some ways to both. Like Wiesel, Fackenheim remains in the dialectic of faith, but he moves beyond story and recognizes that contemporary Jewish life, in its diversity, is the locus of fidelity and that a new midrashic framework has emerged counterbalancing annihilation and survival. This framework is shaken by the Holocaust and must be articulated lest the people perish through cynicism and assimilation. The present Jewish community thus becomes a witness to the world of survival and perseverance, and it is in this activity that the story of evil is remembered. On the other hand, Fackenheim refuses Rubenstein's secular option because even secular Jews are within and testify to Jewish survival. The Jewish community is neither split nor irretrievably broken in any ultimate sense; Jewish life continues in an altered and more urgent form. The option that

Rubenstein offers, to see the Jewish Holocaust as a broader experience of the twentieth century, is neither denied nor affirmed; Fackenheim is propelled by the singularity of the Jewish experience both in slaughter and in survival.[22]

IRVING GREENBERG

In an important way, Irving Greenberg encompasses the previous interpretations of the Jewish Holocaust and moves beyond them. Greenberg perceives the Jewish Holocaust both as an indictment of modernity, because of modernity's false universalism and the evil perpetuated under its reign, and as a critique of the Jewish and Christian religions, because they contributed to powerlessness and hatred. Both modernity and religion have not only contributed to the Holocaust; they have essentially passed over its challenge in silence. The message of the victims—to halt the carnage and to reevaluate the dynamics of social and religious life—has fallen on deaf ears.[23]

The recovery of the story and of the meaning of Holocaust, then, is essential to the redirection of modern life. However, this redirection can occur only if the brokenness is acknowledged. For the past two centuries an allegiance has been transferred from the "Lord of History and Revelation" to the "Lord of Science and Humanism," but the experience of the death camps asks whether this new Lord is worthy of ultimate loyalty. "The victims ask that we not jump to a conclusion that retrospectively makes the covenant they lived an illusion and their death a gigantic travesty." At the same time, nothing in the record of secular culture justifies its claim to authority, especially insofar as it provided the setting for mass death. According to Greenberg, the victims ask us above anything else "not to allow the creation of another matrix of values that might sustain another attempt at genocide." The experience of the past and the possibility of the future urges resistance to the absolutization of the secular.[24]

To refuse to absolutize the secular does not, however, allow an escape into the religious sphere. After Auschwitz, we can speak only of "moment faiths," instances when a vision of redemption is present, interspersed with the "flames and smoke of burning children," where faith is absent. Greenberg describes these "moment faiths" as the end of the easy dichotomy of atheist/theist and of the unquestioned equation of faith with doctrine. After the Holocaust, the difference between the skeptic and the believer is frequency of faith, not certitude of position. The rejection of the unbeliever by the believer is literally the denial or attempted suppression of what is within oneself. To live with moment faiths is to live with pluralism and without the superficial certainties that empty religion of its complexity and often make it a source of distrust for the other.[25]

The dialectic of faith is illustrated in contemporary Jewish experience by the establishment of the State of Israel; and Israel, like the Holocaust, takes on an aspect of a formative experience as well. "The whole Jewish people is caught between immersion in nihilism and immersion in redemption," Greenberg suggests, and fidelity in the present means to remain within the dialectic of Auschwitz (the experience of nothingness) and Jerusalem (the political empowerment of a suffering community). If the experience of Auschwitz symbolizes alienation from God and from hope, the experience of Jerusalem symbolizes the presence of God and the continuation of the people. Burning children speak of the absence of all human and divine value; but the survival of Holocaust victims in Israel speaks of the reclamation of human dignity and value. "If Treblinka makes human hope an illusion, then the Western Wall asserts that human dreams are more real than force and facts. Israel's faith in the God of History demands that an unprecedented event of destruction be matched by an unprecedented act of redemption, and this has happened."[26]

It is Greenberg's understanding that the victims of history are now called to refuse victimhood as meaning fidelity to the dead, although he adds the proviso that to remember suffering propels the community to refuse to create other victims.

> The Holocaust cannot be used for triumphalism. Its moral challenge must also be applied to Jews. Those Jews who feel no guilt for the Holocaust are also tempted to moral apathy. Religious Jews who use the Holocaust to morally impugn every other religious group but their own are the ones who are tempted thereby into indifference at the Holocaust of others (cf. the general policy of the American Orthodox rabbinate on United States Vietnam policy). Those Israelis who place as much distance as possible between the weak, passive Diaspora victims and the "mighty Sabras" are tempted to use

Israeli strength indiscriminately (i.e., beyond what is absolutely inescapable for self-defense and survival), which is to
risk turning other people into victims of the Jews. Neither
faith nor morality can function without serious twisting of
perspective, even to the point of becoming demonic, unless
they are illuminated by the fires of Auschwitz and
Treblinka.[27]

As we can see, within Greenberg's theological perspective the
dialectic of Holocaust and political empowerment is crucial: the
first expressed in Auschwitz, symbol of nothingness; the latter in
Jerusalem, portent of redemption. But Greenberg's dialectic is
broader and more nuanced: the experience of the death camps is a
critique of false religion and of theological language as well as of
political and technological developments within the modern secular world. It enjoins us to do acts of loving kindness and to refuse
that matrix of values and institutions that support genocide. Israel,
as a manifestation of political empowerment, is a symbol of fidelity
to those who perished. The counterpoint is the possibility that
Israeli values and power may undermine that very sign Israel seeks
to be to the Jewish community and the world. If for Greenberg the
dialectic of Holocaust and political empowerment is the foundation of the struggle to be faithful, both poles of the dialectic are
shadowed by the haunting possibility of betrayal.

THE HOLOCAUST AS A UNIVERSAL CRISIS

In the contemporary Jewish experience, then, fidelity to the
Holocaust revolves around the themes of remembrance, critique,
and affirmation, all three sought within a broken world. Complexity and diversity are recognized, and though the crisis engendered
by the Holocaust demands unambiguous answers, such answers
are not easily attained. The emergence of the State of Israel is an
example of this difficulty. From the vantage point of the Holocaust, the political empowerment of the Jewish community cannot
be denied as an essential form of fidelity to the dead. Empowerment, though, especially in the form of a state, places the community in an obvious dilemma: the desire to nurture life and
community is often frustrated by the demands of national security
in a hostile environment. We are also beginning to learn that entry

into history as a powerful community can lead to either fidelity to, or abuse of, the formative event that is the justification for the community's existence.

Having emerged from the prospect of annihilation, the Jewish community thus has entered a present that offers both fruitful possibility and danger. The formative event of the Holocaust can serve to legitimate or to critique power; what we do with that event will determine how the desire to be faithful works itself out concretely in history. The road taken will be the ultimate criterion of fidelity, for if the struggle to be faithful is open to the future, it is yet constrained by the memory of the suffering.

For the Christian, the Jewish Holocaust is no less challenging. Whether in Nazi Germany, Poland, or dozens of other countries, the persecutors were often Christians. Though it is inappropriate to label any of these movements authentically Christian, the symbolic formation and reservoir of hatred that allowed Jews to be isolated, and finally destroyed, owes much to a millennium of Christian anti-Semitism (see note 4, this chapter). If this were not enough, the institutional Church at that great moment of crisis sought self-preservation rather than the commitment demanded to mend a history covered with blood. However, there were Christians willing to place their lives in jeopardy to provide refuge from evil. Though small, this witness allows the question of the validity of Christian faith and activity to remain before us today.[28]

Unfortunately, few Christians have contemplated the haunting difficulty raised by the Jewish Holocaust: What does it mean to be a Christian when Christian understandings and actions issued in the death camps of Nazi Germany? The first response of those who have authentically confronted this evil is to ask forgiveness of the Jewish people and seek forgiveness from Jesus, himself a Jew, whose essential message of love was betrayed. The second response is to remain in dialogue with the experience of Holocaust as a formative event for Christians as well. For to recognize the reality of the death camps and of Christian complicity involves a questioning of the authenticity of Christian faith and activity. Only by realizing and admitting how their conduct denied true Christianity can Christians both salvage and reconstruct their faith. Only by entering into the nothingness of the death camps can a contemporary Christian way of life become authentic. This is what Johannes Metz, the German Catholic theologian, means when he writes,

"We Christians can never go back behind Auschwitz; to go beyond Auschwitz is impossible for us by ourselves. It is possible only together with the victims of Auschwitz."[29]

What of those born Jewish or Christian whose faith has been torn away within or in response to the Holocaust? The experience of dislocation and death has caused a great crisis in belief. The response is either a passion to transform the world so as to prevent injustice and indiscriminate torture or, more often, a numbness and passivity resulting in cynicism. Is it not correct to say that, just as the Jewish and Christian sensibilities are found wanting in the Kingdom of Death, so, too, is the humanist tradition that carries the secular hope of the twentieth century? As noted earlier, it is the very advances of modern life that contributed to the building and activities of the death camps. Like the two major religious traditions of the West, Judaism and Christianity, the humanist tradition became immersed in a formative event that challenged its interpretation of life. While some can remain in the framework that includes both faith and human concern, vast numbers of people cannot continue in that dialectic and are now either passively accepting their fate or consciously, through cynicism and power, causing others to suffer. For those divorced from religious sensibilities, can the Holocaust help them form an active and reflective orientation toward the world in which we live?

These difficult questions must await further clarification. Jewish thinkers are courageous in their ability to face the unknown, although in a sense they have no choice but to face the darkness. Whatever their conclusions, grappling with the horrific signals the desire to be faithful to the experience of the Jewish people. As a whole, Christians and humanists have not honestly addressed the terror of systematic annihilation and what it means for their faith and their worldview. For many, the experience of the Jews is too bothersome to contemplate or is relegated simply to the dustbin of history, as if an enterprise 1,900 years in the making, which issued in its most horrific form only forty-five years ago, is already archaic.

Of course, difficulties glibly addressed or passed over in silence do not disappear, but await rediscovery and interpretation. Awaiting clarity, we travel a path of ignorance toward a destination unknown, a destination that, more often than not, becomes recognizable in the form of nightmare.

CHAPTER 2

The Cost of Empowerment

Immersion in the Holocaust event represents a critique of twentieth-century religion and humanism in both the theoretical and the practical realms; it demands a rethinking of where we have come from and where we are going. In one sense, the Holocaust is a Christian and Western inheritance, and its victims cry out for justice. Yet, in another sense, the Jewish community carries forth this memory and therefore has a special task: to be faithful.

The Jewish writers analyzed earlier pose the question of fidelity in the stark terms of the Holocaust memory, the survival of a decimated people, and Jewish political empowerment in the State of Israel. The price now, however, seems prohibitive. The rise of the neoconservative movement in North America, with its visible and articulate Jewish component exemplified by Norman Podhoretz, editor of *Commentary* magazine, and Irving Kristol, co-editor of *Public Interest,* as well as the ascendancy to power in Israel of religious and secular expansionists, exemplified by Rabbi Meir Kahane, member of the Israeli Parliament, and Ariel Sharon, former Minister of Defense, begins to cloud the horizon. Jewish political empowerment is confronted by the marginalized of the North American continent: Blacks, Hispanics, Native Americans, women. An ever-growing displaced Palestinian people challenges the integrity of the State of Israel. The desire to remain a victim is evidence of disease; yet to become a conqueror after having been a victim is a recipe for moral suicide. It is not too much to claim that the acquired values of the Jewish people, discovered and hammered out over a history of suffering and struggle, are in danger of dissipation. In our liberation, our memory of slavery is in danger of being lost. This loss would allow us to forget what it means to be oppressed. Yet to forget one's own oppression is to open the possibility of becoming the oppressor.

Within the Jewish community the discussion is heated, often framed in terms of struggle rather than debate. The voices are starkly disparate: views of our history, perceptions of our future are sometimes diametrically opposed. That the future of our people is in jeopardy is clear, as is the fact that one or the other's view might lead to disaster. Representative voices of this heated struggle are Irving Greenberg, Nathan and Ruth Ann Perlmutter, Earl Shorris, and Roberta Strauss Feuerlicht.

IRVING GREENBERG

Irving Greenberg's most recent analysis of contemporary Jewish life illustrates this struggle for survival and witness in the theological realm. Having named the Holocaust and its implications, Greenberg embarks on an ambitious, perceptive, and troubling exploration of what he labels "the third great cycle" in Jewish history. While Greenberg attempts to address the difficult realities of Holocaust and empowerment, the limitations of his analysis define the task of Jewish theologians to come.[1]

For Greenberg, Jewish history can be divided into three eras: the Biblical, the Rabbinic, and the present, still unnamed, but which emphasizes the hiddenness of God or Holy Secularity.

The Biblical era represents the formation of the Jewish people, particularly their liberation from slavery and the developing covenantal relationship between God and the people. This was not an easy era by any means. For Greenberg, the difficulty of the period lay in trying to uphold covenantal values in the context of Jewish political sovereignty. When the leaders of the people failed in this task, the prophets arose. Along with the development of the cultic priesthood surrounding the Temple, the Biblical era was marked by a high degree of divine intervention. God's presence in the Temple was the cultic counterpart of prophecy. God spoke directly to Israel through the prophets, and at Jerusalem the divine could be contacted. Thus, for Greenberg, the Biblical period represents a growing sense of mission, with divinity and holiness being expressed in cult and prophecy: Jewish leadership reflects the "active intervention of the divine in Jewish life as well as the struggle to live with the tensions between the covenant and realpolitik."[2]

The destruction of the Second Temple and the crushing defeats of the Jews in 70 and 135 C.E. generated a major crisis of faith and meaning in the Jewish people that ultimately ushered in the Rabbinic era. The tremendous loss of life, the sale of thousands of Jews into slavery, and the triumph of Rome despite the conviction of the Jewish people that God alone should rule Israel deepened the questions. "Was there not God? Had God been overpowered by the Roman gods? Had God rejected the covenant with Israel and allowed his people and the Holy Temple to be destroyed? Were the traditional channels of divine love, forgiveness and blessing now closed to the Jewish people?"[3]

The destruction of the Temple was devastating, for many could no longer envision Judaism without the Temple. At the same time, what was left of Jewish sovereignty disappeared as physical dispersion was complemented by increasing exposure to the cosmopolitan sophistication of Hellenic culture. The rabbis responded by emphasizing Torah study. By internalizing the teachings and values of God's way, the Jews were thus able to compensate in part for the absence of the Temple and the loss of national sovereignty. Greenberg sees the rabbis as engaged in a fundamental theological breakthrough: as manifest divine presence and activity were being reduced, the covenant was actually being renewed. Instead of rejecting the Jews, God had called them to a new stage of relationship and service. In the view of the rabbis, God had withdrawn and become more hidden to allow humans more freedom and a higher level of responsibility, even of partnership, in the covenant, albeit in a newly secular world.

> A world in which God is more hidden is a more secular world. Paradoxically, this secularization makes possible the emergence of the synagogue as the central place of Jewish worship. In the temple, God was manifest. Visible holiness was concentrated in one place. A more hidden God can be encountered everywhere, but one must look and find. The visible presence of God in the Temple gave a sacramental

quality to the cultic life of the sanctuary. Through the High Priest's ministrations and the scapegoat ceremony, the national sins were forgiven and a year of rain and prosperity assured. In the synagogue, the community's prayers are more powerful and elaborate than the individuals' but the primary effect grows out of the individual's own merits and efforts. One may enter the synagogue at all times without the elaborate purification required for Temple entrance because sacredness is more shielded in the synagogue. In the Temple, God spoke directly, through prophecy. In the synagogue, God does not speak. The human-divine dialogue goes on through human address to God. Prayer, which we view today as a visibly sacred activity, was by contrast with the Temple worship, a more secular act. Prayer became the central religious act because of the silence of God.[4]

The rabbis represent a more secular leadership than do priests or prophets. Priesthood was inherited and ritually circumscribed; the rabbis achieved their status through learning, and their sacramental duties were no different from those of the average Jew. If prophets spoke the unmediated word of God, the rabbis used the record of God's instruction to help guide the community in the present. In fact, for the rabbis, prophecy ended with the destruction of the Temple and the exile. How could there be prophecy if God had withdrawn? As Greenberg writes, "Prophecy is the communicative counterpart of splitting the Red Sea! Rabbinic guidance is the theological counterpart of a hidden God."[5]

The characteristics of the Rabbinic era thus come into view. The rabbis were able to interpret the meaning of Jewish fate, to assure the people that the covenant was not broken, to broaden the understanding of and participation in holiness. In essence, they interpreted the meaning of the new Jewish condition of powerlessness and exile and created a unity out of a condition of relative political powerlessness. The hiddenness of God, the synagogue as institutional center, and leadership by the rabbis gave coherence to the second era of Jewish history.

The third era of Jewish history begins with the Holocaust and the crisis of faith and meaning that follows. The covenant of redemption is shattered, and the individual and communal response to that shattering, especially in the building of the State of Israel, is shaping the third era. The third era starts with a series of questions: "Does the Holocaust disprove the classic teaching of redemption? Does Israel validate it [the classic teaching of redemption]? Does mass murder overwhelm divine concern? How should we understand the covenant after such a devastating and isolating experience?" For Greenberg the answer lies in activities that heal the brokenness of the Jewish people rather than in a spoken theology. Jews are called to a "new secular effort to recreate the infinite value of the human being" and in this effort to testify to the hope that a hidden relationship to God's presence still exists. Ultimately it is a call to a new level of covenantal responsibility.[6]

> If God did not stop the murder and the torture, then what was the statement made by the infinitely suffering Divine Presence in Auschwitz? It was a cry for action, a call to humans to stop the Holocaust, a call to the people Israel to rise to a new, unprecedented level of covenantal responsibility. It was as if God said: "Enough, stop it, never again, bring redemption!" The world did not heed that call and stop the Holocaust. European Jews were unable to respond. World Jewry did not respond adequately. But the response finally did come with the creation of the State of Israel. The Jews took on enough power and responsibility to act. And this call was answered as much by so-called secular Jews as by the so-called religious. Even as God was in Treblinka, so God went up with Israel to Jerusalem.[7]

To be sure, the new covenantal mandate challenges more traditional understandings of Jewish faith, for the rabbinic world of synagogue and prayer is no longer adequate. The move from powerlessness to power represents a decisive change in the Jewish condition. The resources, energy, and spirit necessary to create a Jewish state flow in a novel direction. Building the earthly Jerusalem comes first, and the "litmus test of the classic religious ideas becomes whether they work in real life and whether a society can be shaped by them."[8]

For Greenberg the movement toward power is historically inescapable in the face of the Holocaust; Jewish powerlessess is immoral, for it is no longer compatible with Jewish survival. Since the power needed for survival in the contemporary world is available only to sovereign states, achieving power in Israel reaches the level of sacred principle. According to Greenberg, "Any principle that is generated by the Holocaust and to which Israel responds . . . becomes overwhelmingly normative for the Jewish people." Arguing about how power is used is acceptable if the argument does not threaten the Jewish possession of power. How to use the power is the critical point, but endangering the power is the unforgivable sin. In an era oriented by the Holocaust and Israel, such a denial is the "equivalent of the excommunicable sins of earlier eras: denying the Exodus and the God who worked it in the Biblical age or denying the Rabbis and separating from Jewish fate in the Rabbinic era."[9]

At the same time, Greenberg understands that power, being pragmatic and results-oriented, will test the ability of the tradition to advance values and community. Can Jewish ideals be actualized in the world, or are they empty spiritual generalities? Pragmatism rather than the prophetic, compromise rather than perfection, will be the norm in the third era. For Greenberg this shift to pragmatism and compromise signals the end of the traditional Jewish presence on the radical end of the political spectrum, a presence that reflected not only the community's humanitarian concerns, but also its lack of power. The use of power involves compromise and conservation as well as reform and perfection. Guilt and partial failures are inevitable. Despite the fact that power corrupts, it nonetheless must be assumed. For Greenberg, then, the test of morality is a relative reduction of evil and improved mechanisms of self-criticism, correction, and repentance. "There is a danger that those who have not grasped the full significance of the shift in the Jewish condition will judge Israel by the ideal standards of the state of powerlessness, thereby not only misjudging but unintentionally collaborating with attempted genocide. Ideal moral stances applied unchanged to real situations often come out with the opposite of the intended result."[10]

This new pragmatism allows the "occasional use of immoral strategies to achieve moral ends," and Jews must accept this as the price of empowerment. However, in Greenberg's view, power must constantly be challenged by the memory of our powerlessness lest we become hardened to the suffering of others. It is precisely the memory of the Holocaust that has enabled Israel to be a "responsibile and restrained conqueror." The practical application to the plight of the Palestinians follows. For Greenberg the ideal would be maximum self-government for Palestinians and Arabs as a check on Jewish abuse. However, this arrangement can be accepted only if it does not threaten the existence and security of the Jewish people. "To yield autonomy without overwhelming proof of Palestinian desire to live in peace is to invite martyrdom and morally reprehensible death by genocide. The Palestinians will have to earn their power by living peacefully and convincing Israel of their beneficence or by acquiescing to a situation in which Israel's strength guarantees that the Arabs cannot use their power to endanger Israel."[11]

The third era of Jewish history thus poses two fundamental shifts: the movement from the sacramental to secularity, and from hiddenness and powerlessness to empowerment. Though most obvious in the State of Israel, this third era is no less present in the Diaspora. Despite their minority status, European and North American Jews have become increasingly politically active. This activity, according to Greenberg, arises out of the lessons of the Holocaust and the example of Israel, as well as out of the desire to prevent a repetition of the Holocaust and to preserve Israel. Active involvement rather than "invisibility" represents a fundamental shift in Diaspora self-consciousness: though many may elect to remain in the Diaspora rather than settle in Israel, Greenberg believes that psychologically we are coming to the end of exilic Judaism.[12]

The end of almost two thousand years of exilic Judaism poses the final aspect of the third era, the emergence of new Jewish institutions. The primary third-era institutions arise within and exist to support the State of Israel. The Knesset and the Israeli defense forces are prime examples of institutions that deal pragmatically and competently with contemporary Jewish life. Israeli welfare agencies and private organizations also serve this function in Israel and increasingly in the Diaspora. "Kibbutzim and other settlements absorb Diaspora Jews seeking Jewish expression; problem children are sent to Israeli institutions and orphans to Youth Aliya villages. Israeli universities and yeshivot have become important centers for foreign Jewish students." The Israeli Holocaust memorial center, *Yad VaShem,* represents a new sacred institution of the third era. Though government-sponsored and historical rather than mythic, it provides a place where the memory of the Holocaust is preserved and where acts of mourning can be publicly expressed. For Greenberg, *Yad VaShem* illustrates classic religious values in masked fashion: martyrdom, sacrifice, heroism, saintliness, and continuity. The same is true of *Beit Hatefutsot,* the Diaspora Museum, which Greenberg maintains is not really a museum but a "liturgical recounting and reenacting of the Jewish experience in the Diaspora presented in a secular, pluralist, hidden religious fashion."[13]

The Jewish Federation and United Jewish Appeal are examples of third-era institutions in America because they achieved preeminence by responding to the post-Holocaust/Israel reality. Though critics question the religious content of these institutions, Greenberg believes they have tapped both the moral resources of the Jewish community and that community's desire for survival and empowerment. Their message: "You can respond to the worthlessness of Jewish life in the Holocaust by testifying through giving money to rehabilitate Jewish lives." At the same time, political representation of Jewish interests has increased both within the Federation and the Appeal and in direct lobbying groups such as the American Israel Public Affairs Committee (AIPAC). [14]

Still, American Jews seem uncomfortable with politics, preferring philanthropy and sometimes invisibility. Thus, in Greenberg's view, America's political culture is far less mature than that of Israel. Liberalism and universalist rhetoric, with their refusal to admit of group interests and conflicts, have limited American Jewry's political development. Greenberg wants to promote the growth of Jewish political activity in the United States through networks of Jewish political action. These include the working principle "permanent interests, not permanent friends" and policy recommendations such as upgrading AIPAC and establishing Jewish Political Action Committees (PACs) to further Jewish interests domestically and especially in relation to Israel. Not only are Jewish interests promoted, but the danger is lessened that American Jews who lack experience in governance will play a righteous prophetic role vis-à-vis Israel—that is, "hold it to an unreal moral standard, one it could live up to only by endangering its survival."

Implicit in this political view is the notion that the security of Israel is directly linked to the exercise of United States influence and power and that American Jews have a grave responsibility for influencing the United States toward that goal. In the 1970s and early 1980s, in the shadow of Vietnam and the Yom Kippur war, disillusionment steered American Jewish opinion toward peace initiatives that evidenced a strong idealism in foreign policy and hence a great reluctance to use military force to accomplish foreign-policy objectives. In Greenberg's view, this idealism underestimated the role of power in creating peace: "Good will is truly a force in human society and foreign affairs. But it *operates primarily in the framework of a balance of power*—preferably with rewards for good (i.e., peaceful) behavior and punishment for bad (i.e., counterpeaceful) behavior." The emphasis on good will translated into one-sided pressure for concessions from the West; fortunately, for Greenberg, the American arms build-up, the stationing of medium-range missiles in Europe, and the Strategic Defense Initiative have redressed this balance, and the "proper process of reward and punishment has started up again."[15]

Those who promulgate anti-U.S. or anti-Israeli policies must now be wary of the consequences. For Greenberg the renewal of American power illustrated by increasing pressure on the Russians in Afghanistan, by the expansion of rebel forces in Angola, by the U.S. support of the Contras in Nicaragua and by the U.S. withdrawal from UNESCO portends a breakthrough in the Middle East. Israeli strength and perseverance and American power are the two major keys to peace to the Middle East; and the American Jewish community, in its lobbying for aid to Israel and its ability to block similar aid to Jordan and Syria, as well as in its support for the American arms build-up, plays a pivotal role in securing peace.[16]

The newly forming political attitudes and alliances of American Jewry are seen by some as Judaism without religious content or as a "checkbook Judaism" that substitutes financial support for religious obligation. But for Greenberg the relationship between third-era institutions in America, the memory of the Holocaust, and the survival of Israel moves beyond these labels. Though some have commented that the Jewish Federations' power is a function of their superior access to money, Greenberg argues that they are able to attract money only because they transmit meaning and values and can bestow status. The United Jewish Appeal has been able to offer its donors access to Israeli officials, considered to be on the front line of Jewish self-defense. It is the combination of social appeal and theological and historical relevance that makes this kind of involvement so important. At the same time, one of the Federations' recruiting mechanisms has been tours to Israel and Eastern Europe that recall the role of the Holocaust and of Israel and validate philanthropy and Jewish political self-defense. Greenberg believes that beneath these levels of historical consciousness is "a sense that the covenant and destiny of the Jewish people is being continued through this vehicle. The continual media attention to Israel, even the obsessive focus on condemning Israel in the United Nations, is often seen by givers as the secularized version of the Jew's role as a 'light unto the nations' or as the chosen people, singled out and standing alone, testifying to a world mired in the status quo of power politics and oppression."[17]

Third-era institutions in their secularity and response to empowerment eclipse those institutions that characterized the Rabbinic era, especially the centrality of the synagogue. "By continuing to proclaim the evident sacredness of God and of its own place as it did before the Holocaust and rebirth, the synagogue comes across as too sacramental." At the same time, the pre-Holocaust divisions relating to liturgical and covenantal interpretations that generated into Orthodox, Conservative, and Reform denominations contradict the unity called for today. According to Greenberg, synagogue leadership has reacted defensively to this shift, insisting that the synagogue must remain the center of Jewish life. Often these third-era institutions are opposed by the synagogue leadership.[18]

There is a danger that the synagogue leadership will become the *B'nai Bateyra* of the post-Holocaust period. The *B'nai Bateyra* were members of a group that opposed Rabbi Yohanan ben Zakkai's symbolic transfer of the legal, religious authority of the Temple to the court and academy of Yavneh where new institutions were emerging following the Temple's destruction. In that case, faithfulness and the desire to give the familiar response led to a rear guard opposition that was essentially obstructionist. Eventually, the synagogue and academy won and those who staked their fate on reconstituting the Temple died out. In our time, the danger is compounded in that the Temple was visibly destroyed, encouraging the search for alternative ways of religious expression, whereas the synagogue remains physically intact although its theological and cultural substrata have been fundamentally transformed.[19]

Finally, the third cycle of Jewish history represents an age of renewed revelation, where the covenantal way is undergoing a major reorientation and a new sacred literature is being written. Rather than a discontinuity, the third era represents a continuation of a people who for over 5000 years have found themselves in the throes of history and have sought out meaning and value within history. While the Bible, shaped by the Exodus and the message of redemption, represents the first cycle of Jewish history, and the Talmud, affected by the exile and a new understanding of the human-divine partnership, represents the second cycle, the third cycle is providing its own way of revelation and its own scriptures, albeit in a hidden manner.

> The Scriptures of the new era are hidden. They do not present themselves as Scripture but as history, fact, and, sometimes, as anti-Scripture. Revelation has been successfully obscured thanks to the deep hiddenness of the events and the continuing grip of modern ideas which seemingly cut off human culture from revelation channels. The inherited traditions in Judaism and Christianity that [say] there will be no further revelation, which are defensive and designed to protect them from supercession, also serve to block consciousness of revelation by dismissing it in advance. Yet the Scriptures are being written. They are the accounts that tell and retell the event, draw its conclusions and orient the living. In the Warsaw Ghetto, Chaim Kaplan wrote in his journal: "I will write a scroll of agony in order to remember the past in the future."[20]

Greenberg's analysis elucidates the dialectic of community and empire in the Jewish community today yet often obfuscates it in religious language. His working principle that after the Holocaust "No statement theological or otherwise should be made that would not be credible in the presence of the burning children" is a profound call away from empire to community. While he continually calls for models of restraint—telling us to reject unimpeded power—his drift is unmistakable. Pragmatism, alliances, and power are the new watchwords for an ancient community in a hostile world.

Greenberg argues that the prophetic was nurtured by the coalescence of Jewish values and powerlessness, and that with the exercise of power the prophetic should be deemphasized, for it may at certain moments endanger the community. What Greenberg fails to discern about the prophets is that they were not simply speaking in vague generalities or posing ideals impossible to implement in society; they were speaking, sometimes in poetic, figurative language, at other times in realistic detail, about faults in the community that could not be ignored. The prophets, in their explication of transgressions, were pointing to the potentially disastrous course the community was taking. They were talking about survival in no uncertain terms. However, more than the prophetic seems to be losing ground in Greenberg's argument. The ability to understand another's story and hear another's pain, to recognize the formation of other peoples and their struggle for freedom to be as important as our own and as a legitimate demand upon us—this seems to be nonexistent in Greenberg's analysis.[21]

There is no doubt that Greenberg upholds the right to discuss and criticize within certain parameters. His warnings, though, of excommunication from the Jewish community along with his analysis of prophecy and power, contribute to a fear already deeply imbedded in the Jewish community. The insights and sympathies of our people, even the teachings of our tradition, no matter how much in need of modification, are repressed in order to maintain our recently acquired empowerment and must therefore either exist underground or disappear altogether. If it is true that a totally ethical people cannot survive, it is also true that we may be in danger of becoming a people void of ethics.

Though Greenberg's understandings do not explicitly support a neoconservative political policy, and though he himself may be progressive on social issues, the tendency of his theology is to provide a theological foundation for the neoconservative movement within the Jewish community. And Greenberg is not alone here: the political statements of other Holocaust theologians, including Wiesel, Fackenheim, and Rubenstein, display the same tendency. The dynamic balance between Holocaust and empowerment found within their analyses of the Holocaust is lost when they enter the realities of the post-Holocaust world. Empowerment, almost without restraint, becomes the watchword. Greenberg's analysis of the State of Israel as *the* answer to the Holocaust, as *the* sign of deliverance, as *the* redemption out of nothingness, destroys the balance. The Jewish people recently liberated from the hell of Nazi Germany can become, in some minds, reluctant heroic warriors charting the historic course of redemption in a hostile world. Though the forms of oppression vary, the world remains essentially the same—hostile to Jewish interests and survival.[22]

NATHAN AND RUTH ANN PERLMUTTER

For Nathan and Ruth Ann Perlmutter the post-Holocaust world can be explored by examining the shifting nature of anti-Semitism. In their book *The Real Anti-Semitism in America,* the Perlmutters agree that a significant number of Americans still accept the stereotypes of shrewd Jewish business persons and the conspiratorial theories about Jewish bankers, but the financial status of American Jews and the strength of Israel mitigate the effects of this more traditional form of anti-Semitism. The important anti-Semitism of the moment is found in the political arena among those who advance policies inimical to the Jewish community in the United States and the State of Israel.

The United Nations is one such example, especially in its equation of Zionism with racism, which the Perlmutters label as "our time's Big Lie." According to the Perlmutters, the United Nations is a hotbed of anti-Semitism in language and activity. They cite a speech delivered by a Jordanian delegate in 1980 which, among other things, invoked the infamous "protocols of the Elders of Zion," a forged document that speaks of a Jewish international conspiracy to rule the world. At its conclusion there was silence. "The delegate from France, birthplace of liberty, fraternity and equality, said nothing. The delegate from West Germany, a nation which has labored mightily to distance itself from its unspeakable past, sat silently. President Carter's delegate, himself no stranger to racism, deepened the silence with his silence. Not a murmur of protest . . . from anyone . . . save the Israeli ambassador." For the Perlmutters the surprise was not the anti-Semitic tirade but the lack of response from other delegates. The reason for the silence was the national interest of maintaining friendly relations with the Arab OPEC nations. It was as if the expedient silence of the diplomats was a message to Jews saying, "You have been abused, and while our silence is our complicity, really, it's nothing personal."[23]

The Perlmutters' thesis is that Jewish interests are beset by realpolitik as much as by the more familiar anti-Semitic diatribes. Revolutionary governments and movements supported by left-leaning Jewish and non-Jewish intellectuals have often provided the model of this realpolitik, which is essentially anti-Jewish. According to the Perlmutters, the major revolutionary causes since the 1960s—Cuba, Nicaragua, El Salvador, Vietnam, and Iran— have produced new forms of tyranny that the left originally opposed. As important to the Perlmutters is a fundamental shift: many of these revolutionary movements are now allied with the "colonialist Soviet Union or at least with the Jew-hating Yasser Arafat." The Perlmutters conclude that today's revolutionary governments have all too often aligned themselves against the United States, alongside the Soviet Union, or with Arab powers. In the United Nations they contribute to the voting margins of victory for enemies of Israel.[24]

This is also true on the U.S. scene, where traditional liberal allies such as Blacks argue for a quota system that is harmful to Jewish interests and increasingly show pro-PLO sentiments harmful to Israel. Though the Perlmutters wrote their book before the 1984 presidential campaign, where Jesse Jackson emerged as a national Black leader and his "Hymietown" remarks became national headlines, Jackson is mentioned as a part of the Black leadership that is increasingly anti-Jewish in its attitudes and pronouncements.[25]

Old friends slip away and new alliances are formed. For example, in the past, liberal Protestantism showed more tolerance toward Jews than did other groups, but increasingly its political stances, especially in the National Council of Churches, have dam-

aged Israel. The intolerance of fundamentalists, who are traditional enemies of the Jews, is currently "not so baneful as its
friendship for Israel is helpful," and thus a new alliance is possible.
The Perlmutters' description of the National Council of Churches,
like their analysis of the United Nations, finds a wide resonance
among Jewish neoconservatives. Citing the silence of the National
Council during the Six-Day War in 1967 and its immediate con-
demnation of Israel for its occupation of the West Bank soon after,
and the selection of the "anti-Semite" Imamu Baraka, formerly
LeRoy Jones, to be their principal speaker at the Triennial General
Assembly in 1972, the Perlmutters demonstrate a pattern of betrayal. Two other incidents confirm their understanding. According to the Perlmutters, the National Council of Churches did little
better during the Yom Kippur War and the United Nations resolution equating Zionism with racism.[26]

For the Perlmutters, fundamentalist Christian groups that have
long held anti-Semitic views are now in the vanguard of pro-Israel
sentiment and thus need to be courted. This means a reversal of
long-held Jewish views toward fundamentalist Protestants, or at
least a tolerance toward disparate views on the bottom-line support
of the State of Israel. Fundamentalist views on abortion, the Equal
Rights Amendment, prayer in the public schools, and pornography
need to be overlooked or fought in a different arena. Jews, like all
groups, have different convictions on many issues and will continue to express those views even when differing with allies who
agree on the subject of Israel. But for the Perlmutters, not all the
issues are of equal importance. The security of the State of Israel is
far more crucial than the issues on which fundamentalists and Jews
differ. "The conservative fundamentalists today are friends indeed, because unlike the National Council of Churches' liberal
Protestants, they have been friends in need."[27]

The Perlmutters' analysis is increasingly held by American Jews
and is the one most available through media and from Jewish
institutions such as the Anti-Defamation League of B'nai Brith, for
whom Nathan Perlmutter works. It is in a sense a logical extension
of Greenberg's theological work—one way of looking at the post-
Holocaust world. However, there also exists an articulate and
active minority that is critical of such views and seeks to reestablish
the prophetic and ethical dimensions of the Jewish community.

EARL SHORRIS AND ROBERTA STRAUSS FEUERLICHT

Two recent studies are important here: *Jews Without Mercy: A Lament,* by Earl Shorris, and *The Fate of the Jews: A People Torn Between Israeli Power and Jewish Ethics,* by Roberta Strauss Feuerlicht. Both reflect on Jewish history and ethics as a means to criticize the present.

For Earl Shorris, Jewish history is one of woes and contribution: "Suffering and philosophy, poverty and poetry, exile and community, tears and mercy are all intertwined in Jewish history." Though Jews are diverse in time periods, interests, and definitions—whether ghetto Jews or early Zionists, universalists or assimilationists—historically a commonality could be found in the ethical and historical basis of Judaism: "Whatever the subtle differences in interpretation of the yoke of the Law, the ethical basis of the Law remained. Judaism was the first ethical religion, the first ethical civilization, and so it remains, even to the assimilationists, who are willing to give up everything but the ethics of their fathers." However, to Shorris, the new definition of Jewish interests put forward by the Jewish neoconservative movement differs from previous definitions. He begins by outlining their fundamental analysis.[28]

Blacks betrayed the Jews, the very people who helped them up out of racism and poverty into their current situation. Blacks are anti-semitic. Jews should not help Blacks anymore, nor should they help other minorities, such as Hispanics, because they will only turn on the Jews as the Blacks did. . . .

The State of Israel can do no wrong.

The Palestinian people have no right to exist as a state, nor do Palestinian territorial claims have any validity.

The killing of an Israeli civilian by a Palestinian is an act of terrorism.

The killing of a Palestinian civilian by an Israeli is a justifiable act of self-defense.

Occupation and colonization of foreign territory by Israel is not imperialism.

Any political position taken by an American Jew is justified if it can be associated with the survival of Israel. . . .

The poor of America are wretches without dignity. They constitute an underclass that it is best to neglect, for only through the rigors of necessity can they achieve dignity in the last decades of the twentieth century as the Jews did in the first decades of this century.[29]

This leads Shorris to a series of questions which are, at the same time, a lament:

The new definition of Jewish interests belongs to an arrogant people. How can it belong to a small and humble people? The new definition belongs to a selfish people. How can it belong to a people who have been instructed to be "a light to the nations"? The new definition belongs to a people of unlimited power and no history. How can it belong to a people who remember that they were "sojourners in Egypt"? One can understand how Jews could fear the outside world or wish for a homeland or wish to disappear safely into another culture or seek the good life for all so that they might enjoy it as well. The new definition has the chill of loneliness about it. The expressions of it are sometimes grasping, sometimes combative, sometimes vengeful.[30]

Shorris' descriptions lead to important questions he does not shirk: Are not those who take these neoconservative positions fundamentally changing the definition of what it means to be Jewish? Are those who adhere to these positions on social issues really justified in claiming to be Jewish? Or are they searching out a new religion that is something other than Judaism?

Roberta Strauss Feuerlicht also addresses the drift in the Jewish community, but from an even more critical angle. Like Shorris, Feuerlicht sees the essential heritage of the Jewish people as bound up with the ethical imperative. For Feuerlicht, the heritage of the Jews is not power but ethics: "Whether Jews are a religion, a people, a civilization, a historical process, or an anomaly, whether they are Hasidim or heretics, what binds all Jews from antiquity to the present is not statehood but the burden they placed upon themselves and posterity when they internalized morality and gave the world the ethical imperative."[31]

Yet more often than not, Jews have violated that imperative. For example, Jews were slave owners and slave traders. The golden age of Jewry in Spain owed some of its wealth to an international network of Jewish slave traders where Bohemian Jews purchased Slavonians and sold them to Spanish Jews for resale to the Moors. In the American South before the Civil War, a disproportionate number of Jews were slave owners, slave traders and slave auctioneers. When the line was drawn between the races, by and large Jews were on the white side.[32]

Though many Jews worked in the Civil Rights movement of the 1950s and 1960s, more recent Black-Jewish relations have been characterized by a Jewish posturing that borders on arrogance. For Feuerlicht, the Andrew Young affair, which began with a meeting with representatives of the PLO and ended in Young's dismissal as the U.S. representative to the United Nations in August 1979, illustrates the problem. According to Feuerlicht the Jewish establishment never liked Young because of his gift for the controversial and his pronounced bias toward the Third World, which in Jewish terms meant that he was an enemy of Israel. Jewish leaders believed that Young was one of the Jimmy Carter insiders who tilted the U.S. president toward the Arab world. And yet Young was the only powerful Black in government and thus a symbol of progress and hope for the Black community.

Young's resignation thus introduced a new phase in Black-Jewish relations. Black leaders were angered by the statements of Jewish leaders suggesting that Blacks had no right to comment on Mideast affairs. Within a week of Young's resignation, Black leaders met with PLO representatives at the United Nations. As a result, Southern Christian Leadership Conference president Reverend Joseph Lowery endorsed the "human rights of all Palestinians, including the right to self-determination in regard to their own homeland." Yehuda Blum, Israel's chief UN delegate, criticized Black leaders for supporting a Palestinian homeland, commenting, "Understandably, they are less knowledgeable about the Middle East conflict than other parties." Lowry replied, "We make no apologies for our support of human rights for Palestinians." Afterward the Black leaders went to the American Jewish Congress and met with Jewish leaders who said it was "a grave error" for the Blacks to meet with the PLO. One Black minister said, "There will be no peace in the Middle East until justice comes to the Palestinians. All you have to do is visit a refugee camp one time and you will know that the Palestinians are the niggers of the Middle East."[33]

Feuerlicht, like Shorris, confronts the most controversial issue, the State of Israel. Though she admits historical reasons for the state and supports its continued existence because of the now-resident Jewish population, Feuerlicht believes that no further movement toward justice can take place without an honest look at its development. For Feuerlicht, the Zionists chose to create a state by imposing on an indigenous population and culture descendants of Jews from all over the world who had not lived there in any significant number for thousands of years and who shared little except their Jewish identification. Because Israel was imposed upon the indigenous population by a nonresident people, Feuerlicht sees the state as a form of colonialism, not of liberation. She quotes Professor Israel Shahak, chairman of the Israeli League for Human and Civil Rights, who said of Israeli development "that almost 400 Arab villages were completely destroyed, with their houses, garden-walls, and even cemeteries and tombstones, so that literally a stone does not remain standing, and visitors are passing and being told that it was all the desert." She also quotes Moshe Dayan, who once said, "We came to this country which was already populated by Arabs, and we are establishing a Hebrew, that is a Jewish state here. Jewish villages were built in the place of Arab villages. There is not one place built in this country that did not have a former Arab population."[34]

In many ways this policy of expropriation and denial of Palestinian rights continues today, especially in the occupied territories. Palestinians have been forced into a dependency on Israeli corporations and government through expropriation of their land and a conscious policy of underdeveloping the Palestinian economic infrastructure. Palestinians are discriminated against in employment, education, and land use. Resisting these injustices can result in blacklisting and arrest, often without legal remedy. Once Palestinians are imprisoned, brutality and torture are commonplace. Feuerlicht cites Felicia Langer, an Israeli attorney and human rights activist, who has reported on West Bank prisons. Describing crowded prison conditions, bad food, and inadequate medical care, Langer writes that prisoners are also beaten and tortured. Langer's conclusion: "Prisoners are being put to death. . . . This crime is occurring gradually and is being covered up efficiently."[35]

Through these and other policies, Israel fosters an internal colonialism that in Feuerlicht's view creates an interesting though tragic twist to Jewish history. For centuries Jews lived as an exiled people. Denied rights and privileges, they were forced into certain occupations by discriminatory laws. When certain rights were granted Jews in the eighteenth and nineteenth centuries, they were granted to individuals, not to the Jewish people. As the French philosopher Clermont-Tonnerre wrote, "Everything should be denied to the Jews as a nation; everything should be granted to them as individuals." The continuing policy that Israel will give Arabs rights as individuals but not as a nation strikes Feuerlicht as ironic. The editorial in *Ha'aretz,* an Israeli newspaper, which states that though this "is not optimal from a national point of view" it is the "maximum they can expect as a minority" saddens Feuerlicht, for to her mind the Israelis have made the Arabs the Jews of Israel.[36]

In some ways, the Israeli invasion of Lebanon in June 1982 is an extension of this internal colonialism. The atrocities committed by the Israeli military are well documented, and Feuerlicht cites the July 18, 1981, bombing of Beirut, almost a year before the official invasion began, as a reflection of the brutality with which Arabs within Israel are treated. Though the bombing was ostensibly conducted to strike terrorists' targets, most of the buildings demolished in that bombing were apartment houses. More than three hundred civilians were killed. To a *Washington Post* query, the Israeli chief of military intelligence responded that the motive of Israel's bombing raids in Beirut was to generate Lebanese civilian resentment against the presence of Palestinian guerrillas. A few days later, Israeli bombers again struck Lebanon. Feuerlicht cites the *New York Times,* which reported that witnesses, including Western reporters caught in the attacks, said that nearly all the casualties were civilians, some of them burned alive in their cars, trapped in clogged traffic.[37]

In spite of her analysis, Feuerlicht concludes that Israel must continue to exist because the alternative would mean another holocaust. However, if Israel continues on its present course, it will be morally bankrupt and the ethical imperative, the foundation of Jewish life, will be smashed. In a startling and controversial conclusion Feuerlicht writes: "Judaism as an ideal is infinite; Judaism as a state is finite. Judasim survived centuries of persecution without a state; it must now learn how to survive despite a state."[38]

And yet for Feuerlicht, as for Shorris, Jews carry forth the often-defeated ethical ideal, an ethical imperative derived from Moses and the prophets, and from our history of fidelity and martyrdom. Often this has placed Jews in a position of exile within the nations of the world; today it increasingly demands an exilic posture within the Jewish community itself. This is a difficult and unexpected place for a Jew, especially after the Holocaust. Such an awakening, however, might provide the physical and psychological space to develop critical insights and activity that call the Jewish people to pursue ethical rather than oppressive power.

Thus Shorris and Feuerlicht pose critical questions to Greenberg and the Perlmutters. If it is true that the new scriptures, the scrolls of agony written with bitterness and hope, come from the ghettos of eastern Europe, are not similar scrolls being written today by Lebanese and South African women and men and their "burning children"? The global economic system, of which the United States is the most powerful and from which many Jews benefit, reinforces a form of triage that translates into millions of malnourished and starving children. Can we continue to mourn our dead and at the same time refuse to act as if these are not "burning children"? In the eyes of the Palestinians, expansionist Israel, linked to U. S. military and economic support, is the empire against which it struggles. If heard at all, their story is secondary. Can we expect Guatemalan and Salvadoran peasants to understand the Jewish struggle for empowerment when Israeli arms sales and military training support the ever-growing landscape of death littered with orphaned children? Can we honestly say that critiquing Israel's participation in the equipping of Somoza's forces before the Nicaraguan revolution, or Israel's continuing contributions to the scientific, military, and economic interests of South Africa, or the wholesale expropriation of Palestinian land on the West Bank and Gaza, is the role of the prophet in the Jewish community? And further, that such questions need to be silenced in the third era of Jewish history? For Shorris and Feuerlicht, the third-era sacred institutions, *Yad VaShem* and *Beit Hatefutsot,* may relate our scroll of agony but increasingly neglect the scrolls scripted today. Will not this other side of our history be recorded and one day become part of the scripture we are forced by conscience to recite to our children?[39]

From this critical posture, Feuerlicht and Shorris believe that we can begin to name the new forms of idolatry the Jewish community has embraced: capitalism; nationalism; survival at any cost. Their critique of the Jewish community may lift us beyond the dialectic of Holocaust and empowerment to a reasoned understanding of the dilemmas of Jewish life and the choices before us as a community. It may also open a path of generosity toward other struggling communities and decrease our new-found arrogance and our consequent isolation from liberation movements around the globe. We have inherited a history of anguish and possibility. What history shall we bequeath to our children?

CHAPTER 3

Movements of Jewish Renewal

The tension between empire and community has surfaced in every age. "Empire" goes beyond an individual's attempt to dominate, control, or manipulate others for survival and affluence; it represents the organization of this impulse and the creation of structures that ensure a pattern of dominance and control. "Community" moves in another direction. Equality, cooperation, and mutuality in decision making become the goals, and structures are created that foster creativity rather than domination. Rarely, however, is either empire or community perfectly realized. Where domination is the organizing principle, those who seek community become the way of the future; where community is primary, the will to dominate remains.[1]

In a small but nonetheless intense way we can see how this dialectic of empire and community is being played out in contemporary Jewish life. Though there are many reasons why the Jews have survived in desperate circumstances, it seems that the will to community is preeminent among them. The post-Holocaust world, however, is a unique place with different demands for survival. Many fear the Jewish people cannot survive without empire. Over against this view, many reassert that the values of Jewish life are the Jews' essential witness to the world and that without such a witness, Judaism ceases to be Judaism. The forces of renewal see no choice but to balance the survival of the Jewish people with the preservation of its essential message of community. Those forces assert that

survival and preservation of Judaism's essential message are ultimately one and the same: there is no meaningful survival without a
deepening of the witness its message offers to the world.

At least three renewal movements alive in today's Jewish community are worthy of exploration. They include those who leave
secular outlooks and embrace Jewish movements of social and
political action, and the burgeoning feminist consciousness among
Jewish women. These movements consider seriously the formative
events of our time—the Holocaust and the birth of the State of
Israel—and at the same time pose critical questions about the
direction of Jewish life.[2]

FROM SECULARISM TO JUDAISM

The first movement is comprised of those who, while born
Jewish, have later in life made conscious decisions to become
actively involved in Jewish ritual and ethics. These are "secular"
Jews who have converted to Orthodox or neo-Orthodox Judaism
and are known in Hebrew as *ba'alei-teshuvah,* "those who return."
They have experienced *teshuvah,* the process of repentance for
transgressions and of return to the correct observance of Jewish
ethical and ritual law. The *ba'alei-teshuvah* are a traditional Jewish
category in a new way: since they have lived outside a traditional
Jewish community context, they are not so much returning to an
observance of Jewish law as they are reentering a Judaism with
which they have had little or no acquaintance.[3]

Many of the *ba'alei-teshuvah* are Americans from upper- and
middle-class suburban neighborhoods who helped form the youth
culture of the sixties and seventies. They protested the ethical
decline of American society evidenced in the Vietnam War, racial
conflict, and the emptiness of an affluent and technologically
sophisticated culture. For some, the answer is the exploration and
renewal of a Jewish way of life, and it often occurs within the
context of travel and study. Many find their way to Israel, study in
Jewish houses of learning, and make their lives in a new religious
environment. Others remain in the United States. However, the
journey is quite similar: the feelings of being lost and alienated; the
search for foundations to build a life upon; the joy of discovering
and embracing a way of life that is deeply one's own.[4]

Of those who return, many have led active political lives on the left, with no apparent religious affiliation. They have been propelled by Jewish ethical concern without identifying that concern as Jewish. On their return to Judaism, their political convictions, now permeated with religious categories and visions, are deepened. An example of one who has made such a return to Judaism is Arthur Waskow. For years Waskow was a social activist with little Jewish affiliation. In the 1970s he returned to Judaism to search out a rootedness and community previously neglected—and has emerged as a major Jewish theologian concerned with renewal.[5]

The journey was far from easy, for recovery of his Jewishness necessitated a rigorous study of the tradition's sources, the Torah and Talmud. As Waskow describes it, the sojourn was akin to a *teshuvah* in that it was a radical change of perspective that reoriented his life and thought. His *teshuvah* began in Washington, D.C., ten days after the assassination of Martin Luther King, Jr., and on the eve of Passover. After eighteen hours of racial tension, crowds from the Black community rioted, and food, doctors, and lawyers disappeared from the community. Waskow was part of a network that attempted to bring food to hungry ghetto neighborhoods, doctors to the sick and injured, and lawyers to the jails. Because they were white they were allowed to roam the streets despite the curfew.

Tonight, however, was a time for being home. Tonight would be the beginning of Passover. It was the time for my encounter with the sacred past—the sacred past of the Jewish people, the sacred past of my own family. It was safely "past"—and therefore, *therefore* sacred. A time to recite in high and solemn tones the archaic English of my old *Haggadah*. A time to look again at its old drawings, at the faded inscription that said it was a present for bar mitzvah, at the stains of ancient dribbled wine. A time to leave the turmoil of America, of 1968, of burning streets and napalmed villages, of a murdered saint and murderous presidents. A time for ceremonious pleasure. But not this afternoon. As I walked up Eighteenth Street toward my house, my steps began to drum an eerie sentence:

This is Pharaoh's Army. . . .
And I am on my way to do the Seder.
This is Pharaoh's Army. . . .
And I am on my way to do the Seder.

Block after block, I remembered the words King spoke the night before he died, . . . the words that echoed Moses: "I am standing on the mountain top, looking across into the Promised Land. I may not get there, but my people will." And when I turned the corner at Wyoming Avenue, there it was still: a United States Army jeep, machine gun still pointing vaguely at my house. The rhythmic chant came back again, this time a question:

This is Pharaoh's chariot. . . .
And I am on my way to do the Seder?

The Passover *Haggadah* had come alive to stalk the streets. That night, for the first time, I broke open the form of the Haggadah to talk about the streets and what had been happening to us. For the first time I felt the Seder a moment not for high and solemn recitation, but for burning passion and hard thinking. For the first time, we paused to talk about its meaning.[6]

From this point on, Waskow's social theory and activity proceed from wrestling with the tradition and from the need to articulate its significance for modern life. His hope is for a renewal of Judaism that will release the Jewish community from wandering in alien concepts and struggles and allow it to become fully itself. "Wrestling" with the tradition provides insight into the modern world that contemporary life, by its very nature, lacks.[7]

Waskow's interest in applying the Jewish traditions to modern life is critical. Unlike Greenberg, Wiesel, Fackenheim and Rubenstein, Waskow sees the rabbinic era continuing although evolving into a new configuration. Thus Waskow's theology sees the Holocaust and Israel in a historical continuity rather than as formative events from which Jewish life begins and ends. At the same time, Waskow seeks to integrate modern insights into the rabbinic scheme and believes that an updated Jewish tradition can address the emptiness and evil of modern cultural and political life. For Waskow, Greenberg's third era of Jewish history can become woefully void of traditional Jewish content and might lead to alignments with unjust power. The rabbinic tradition, on the other hand, grounds Jews in a pattern of thought, prayer, and activity that has internal content and is subject to public critique.[8]

Central to the rabbinic tradition is the place of Torah in study and activity, and Waskow believes the Torah represents the "authentic Jewish process for working out how to live." For Waskow the Torah is expansive; it includes the biblical and talmudic traditions as well as rabbinic and modern commentaries on them—even secularist commentaries in dialogue with the biblical and talmudic tradition. The rebirth of Torah discussion found in *havurot,* small Jewish fellowships, means the rediscovery of a common process of argument and activity that has dissipated because of modernity and the Holocaust. This Torah discussion infuses content into Jewish life and provides a foundation for the critique of modern culture, a culture that is univocal in its outlook and therefore often dangerous in its arrogance. Thus the study of Torah has a twofold purpose of addressing the Jewish people and the world.

1. Because the wrestle with Torah is precisely the authentic Jewish process for working out how to live. This is what the prophets did; it is what the rabbis did when they were talking and then writing the Talmud; it is what Kabbalists and Hassidim and Reform Jews and often secular Zionists and Bundists did. It is even apparent that the Torah itself interlaces several strands of wrestling with Torah. And even when different Jews and different groups of Jews have disagreed over what Torah taught, they have stayed together as part of the Jewish people because they shared a common process of argument. In our own generation, when the Jewish people has succeeded in creating institutions with great political clout, it is important to make sure those institutions become and stay seriously Jewish by working out their political positions through struggling with Jewish tradition.

2. Because Torah carries teachings that are crucial if humankind is to survive its present profound crisis and to transform

the world rather than destroy it. What is more, these Torah teachings are different from much of what we find in modern secular ideologies—whether nationalism, liberalism, individualism, socialism, capitalism, science or industrialism. All these ideologies—products of the last four hundred years of human history—have basic flaws if we are seeking guides on how to grow past the crises we are in, because the crises are themselves products of the last four hundred years and of those ideologies.[9]

The application of biblical concepts to modern life is of course difficult. But the process itself encourages new ways of seeing. Waskow's own realization of the importance of the biblical jubilee, for example, came within the context of the U. S. bicentennial celebration in 1976. As the planning for the bicentennial proceeded, Waskow saw two sets of people: officials who were planning fireworks and galas, and populists who saw the global corporations as modern equivalents of the British monarchy. One group of the new populists, the People's Bicentennial Commission, met at the research center where Waskow worked. As they talked about "tea parties" and "economic democracy," he realized that a bicentennial is also a jubilee, so that 1976 should be an American jubilee year. In fact, it should be the fourth American jubilee, but there had been only one in 1865, and this was partial, freeing the slaves but not redistributing the land. In trying to focus attention on the jubilee, Waskow met with some rejections but also with affirmation. Those who affirmed Waskow's sensibility included the Black preacher who recalled his grandfather's telling how it was a jubilee in '65, and who had created his own conference on applying the jubilee to American society; the rabbi who proposed that every family in America be offered a homestead to garden and preserve the land; the neighborhood organizer who realized that Henry George, the great American reformer, had said the jubilee was the root of his proposals for a special tax on speculation and profits in land values; the Catholic priest who proposed that in the holy years, each diocese should forgive the debts owed to it by the poorer parishes; and the theologian who saw the jubilee as an aspect of a North American theology of relinquishment—one that would allow the affluent to achieve reconciliation with the working class and the poor.[10]

As the process continued, Waskow's own sense of the jubilee deepened. In modern thought, religious and spiritual questions are often separated from political and economic issues; the jubilee brings these issues together. It says that to achieve equality the concept of ownership must change, but it adds that the path to spiritual transcendence requires the equal sharing of material goods. Yet the jubilee does not rest on a utopian or a perfectionist sense of human nature. Instead it creates a cycle of change that recognizes the limitations of social and individual life.

In the practical realm, Waskow believes that the jubilee encourages tax reform by way of loans to community-, worker-, and family-run enterprises; decentralized community control over land and housing; production and distribution of food on a socially responsive basis; and individual and communal repose and recreation.[11]

Waskow's sensibilites are fascinating and complex, and justice can hardly be done them here. What is crucial for our understanding, though, is the neo-orthodox strain Waskow displays: a relevant biblical and talmudic tradition is available to us if we take our own tradition seriously. Conversely, a renewal of body and soul leading to wholeness is unavailable to a people set loose from their past. Wholeness, as in the biblical shalom, is impossible without justice.

MOVEMENTS OF SOCIAL AND POLITICAL ACTION

The second movement of renewal within the Jewish community consists of groups who address the specific social and political realities that today's Jews face but with less emphasis on the spiritual roots of Jewish tradition. One such group is the New Jewish Agenda, a movement that brings progressive religious and secular Jews into a community of concern and activity to counteract political and religious neoconservatism. Founded in December 1980, they seek to reaffirm the agenda of the Jewish community in solidarity with those who struggle for justice. Agenda's Statement of Purpose, written in 1982, reflects this goal.

We are Jews from a variety of backgrounds and affiliations committed to progressive human values and the building of a shared vision of Jewish life.

Our history and tradition inspire us. Jewish experience and teachings can address the social, economic, and political issues of our time. Many of us find our inspiration in our people's historical resistance to oppression and from the Jewish presence at the forefront of movements for social change. Many of us base our convictions on the Jewish religious concept of *tikkun olam* (the just ordering of human society and the world) and the prophetic tradition of social justice.

We are dedicated to insuring the survival and flourishing of the Jewish people. Jews must have the rights to which all people are entitled. But survival is only a precondition of Jewish life, not its purpose. Our agenda must be determined by our ethics, not our enemies. We need creative and vital Jewish institutions and practices that affirm the best of our traditions and involve members of our community who have historically been excluded.[12]

The National Platform they adopted includes progressive positions on racism, lesbian and gay rights, and Israel.[13]

In an attempt to carry out their National Platform, Agenda members are politically active both inside and outside of the Jewish community. For instance, in the summer of 1984 New Jewish Agenda organized the Jewish Human Rights Delegation to Nicaragua. The Reagan administration charged that in Nicaragua there exists "Sandinista-sponsored, supported and condoned anti-Semitism." One charge said that the government threatened and harassed members of the Jewish community by confiscating its property and defiling the synagogue. The Anti-Defamation League of B'nai Brith publicly supported the charge; other Jewish groups disputed the claim. A central question was whether the administration was attempting to arouse fears of anti-Semitism in order to rally political support for its anti-Sandinista policy. After meeting in Nicaragua with government officials, representatives of human rights organizations, opposition groups and parties and members of the Nicaraguan Jewish community, the delegation concluded: "Charges of Nicaraguan government anti-Semitism cannot be supported; there simply is no body of credible evidence to suggest that the Sandinista government has pursued or is currently pursuing a policy of discrimination or coercion against Jews, or that Jewish people are not welcome to live and work in Nicaragua."[14]

The following December the first Jewish delegation of Witness for Peace, sponsored by the New Jewish Agenda, arrived in Nicaragua. The twenty participants spent a week in the villages of Somotillo and Achuapo, near the Honduran border where many attacks by the American-backed contras take place. They celebrated Chanukah in Somotillo and in Corinto, the Nicaraguan port town whose harbor has been mined by the CIA. To the question of why they are risking their lives in Nicaragua, they responded in a statement read in front of the American embassy in Managua:

> Our Judaism brings us to this place because our tradition asks us to speak out against injustice. We, as a people, are dedicated to *Tikkun Olam,* the just restitution and repair of the world. Through our tradition, we have accepted the responsibility of preserving the world in our laws, our text, and mostly, our hearts. Forty years ago Jews learned just how unjust people can be to each other. We learned there is no torture beyond comprehension, no reason once the path to destruction is set. We know, as a people, that there is no such thing as an injustice happening to someone else; it happens to us all.[15]

Another political movement of renewal, Oz VeShalom, Religious Zionists for Strength and Peace, comes from within Israel itself. Founded in 1975 as a reaction to the misinterpretation of biblical texts and distortions of religious Zionism, particularly in the promotion of Jewish settlements in the occupied West Bank and Gaza territories, Oz VeShalom wages a political and educational campaign aimed at viewing these territories within a broader moral framework. As Torah-committed Israelis, its members take up the political challenge of calling Jewish citizens back from the path of ethnocentricity and chauvinism.[16]

According to Oz VeShalom, the discussion over the future of the occupied territories is in fact a discussion about the future of the State of Israel. An increasingly popular view of the legitimate application of the Torah to the central issues of Israeli life is represented by Gush Emunim (the "Block of the Faithful"). Its members maintain that the messianic redemption of the Jewish people is linked to "wholeness" of the land of Israel under Jewish-Israeli control. Thus they see the Israeli conquest of the West Bank and Gaza Strip in 1967 as a "divinely-supported liberation of parts of *Eretz Yisrael*." Any return of these territories would be violating the will of God. To prevent this, Gush Emunim has pioneered the establishment of Jewish settlements in the West Bank, creating, as it were, a sense of irreversibility about the occupation.[17]

Oz VeShalom takes a contrary view by seeing the cost of holding on to the disputed territories as too high, if the Jewish state "wishes to remain faithful to Jewish values and *mitzvot* (divinely commanded acts) that pertain to interpersonal and intercommunal relations, not just the people-to-land relationship." Palestinian nationalism means that Israeli rule in the West Bank and Gaza will have to be a rule of force, and this inevitably leads to repression and injustice. Oz VeShalom argues that no theological claims can justify unjust actions and that the Jewish people has suffered greatly in the past from messianic movements that claimed to know God's plan for humanity in any particular generation.

> We Jews have a revealed and revered tradition that teaches us that all human beings, not just Jews, are created in God's image and are worthy of being treated with dignity, respect, and compassion. Being the beneficiaries of such a rich tradition, extending over three and a half millennia, is a "mixed blessing"—for we have teachings in our sacred literature that stem from an ancient era when Jews were the only monotheists around. Applying those teachings to Jewish-Arab relations today, or making wholesale analogies to, say, the book of Joshua, is a very dangerous business. Moreover, the Jewish experience of cultural insularity ("ghettoization") over many centuries did not prepare us for the encounter with Christians and Muslims in our ancestral homeland when our prayers and yearnings during 2,000 years of exile were finally fulfilled. For us to live in peace and security in that cherished

homeland, and to help Jewish culture to flourish by its contact with both the earth and the peoples of the Land, we Israelis must arrive at some kind of political compromise in which human sovereignty over God's Holy Land is shared with our Palestinian neighbors.[18]

Uriel Simon, Professor of Bible at Bar Illan University and a founding member of Oz VeShalom, reiterates this point in the movement's publication of March 1982. For Simon, the basic moral dilemma facing Israel is that the pursuit of peace and justice cannot be reconciled with occupying the West Bank; there is no alternative but to choose between them. It is incumbent upon Israel to relinquish the one value for the greater good of the other, and Simon concludes that the Jewish national movement should not deny the basic right of self-determination to a million Arabs in the occupied territories. "Continuing to hold on to areas of *Eretz Israel* which were occupied in the Six-Day War, and are densely populated by Arabs, must necessarily lead us astray. Rule by force must eventually deteriorate into a regime of oppression. We must not inflict upon others that which is hateful to ourselves."[19]

For Oz VeShalom the choice is clear and the need for action urgent. In the *Jerusalem Post* International Edition, May 23, 1982, they placed the following editorial.

THE CHOICE IS OURS

"I have set before you life and death, blessing and curse: therefore choose life, so that both you and your offspring may live. . . . that you may dwell in the land which the Lord swore unto your forefathers, to Abraham, to Isaac, and to Jacob, to give unto them." Deuteronomy 30:19–20

CITIZENS OF ISRAEL, it is up to us to decide whether we want:

-a Jewish state governed by Biblical values, just laws, and reason

OR -a garrison state characterized by chauvinism, institutionalized injustice, and xenophobia

-a democratic society,	OR	-all of *Eretz Yisrael* at the price of repressing the political freedom of over 1 million Palestinian Arabs
flourishing within smaller borders, in which the Arab minority enjoys full human dignity and civil rights		
-mastery of our collective destiny in harmony with our neighbors	OR	-dependence on the U.S. for the weapons and money needed to wage war
-chances for increasing economic and political cooperation with Europe and the Third World	OR	-growing isolation and condemnation within the world community
-mutual recognition and coexistence between Israelis and Palestinians	OR	-escalating destruction and loss of life

IT CLEARLY TAKES TWO SIDES TO MAKE PEACE, but OUR vision of a Jewish state, and OUR actions in pursuit of that vision, are OUR responsibility. Our children and grandchildren deserve our unceasing efforts to secure for them the blessing of peace.[20]

Within this second movement of renewal there have emerged increasing acts of Jewish civil disobedience. In the United States, civil disobedience takes on a variety of issues, from involvement in Central America to complicity in the arms race. Protested, too, is our continuing tolerance of apartheid in South Africa and the refusal of Soviet authorities to allow Jews to emigrate.

In August 1985, the call to civil disobedience led Phyllis Taylor, a Philadelphia nurse and member of the Jewish Peace Fellowship, to the Nevada desert where nuclear weapons are tested. Taylor was asked to lead the nonviolent training exercises for the August Desert Witness, an ecumenical nonviolent witness commemorating the fortieth anniversary of Hiroshima and Nagasaki. But for Taylor, the event had other meanings as well. "For forty years our ancestors wandered in the desert. Forty years ago Auschwitz and Bergen-Belsen were liberated and the world became aware of the Holocaust."[21]

Another Jewish resistor to nuclear weapons is Todd Kaplan, now serving a three-year sentence in the Federal Prison Camp in Danbury, Connecticut, for his involvement in the actions of the "Pershing Plowshares" group in April 1984. At that time, Kaplan and several others entered the Martin Marietta factory in Orlando, Florida, where the Army's Pershing II intermediate-range ballistic missiles are manufactured. As the group poured their blood and damaged sections of the missiles with hammers, Kaplan blew a shofar as a call of repentance. The group then issued a "Declaration of Conscience, Passover/Easter 1984" that concludes: "We express our desire to repent of the deeper violence that secures power and property while it bankrupts the spirit of a nation pledged to a welcome for the world's oppressed and to life, liberty and happiness for all.[22]

As with Taylor, this was not Kaplan's first act for justice but was rather a continuation of a lifetime of work that includes being a member of a group that serves as advocates for the poor and the homeless in Washington, D.C., as well as work in Jewish/Arab relations in Israel at Neve Shalom, a community that brings Jews and Arabs together to live and dialogue in a nonthreatening atmosphere. It was here at Neve Shalom that Kaplan also tried to find Palestinian prisoners missing during the war in Lebanon.

As a Jew, Kaplan takes seriously the relationship of the Holocaust to nuclear war, and the use of "Torah symbolism" in the Plowshares action symbolizes this connection. In an interview with Alan Mandell in September 1985, Kaplan speaks of Jewish commitment and the mandate from Isaiah to create a peaceful world.

I believe that the elimination of nuclear arms is a goal that we as Jews should embrace and I want to help make this as central to our awareness as it is to our survival. This means that we may have to challenge the rest of the Jewish community in a public way, one that invites criticism and ridicule, but that can also speak strongly of the truth of our situation today. . . . I think we need to take the idea of holocaust prevention both seriously and personally. We, as Jews, can't stand by passively and see the values that we hold dear go down the drain. There is a risk in not doing anything, especially in preventing wars—in particular nuclear wars. And this is really why I went and did the Plowshares action. I believe that it is "holocaust prevention" in the purest sense. This is an act that is possible before it's too late, before our whole planet becomes one huge death camp. You go and start the disarmament process before these weapons disarm us.[23]

Another form of civil disobedience relating to war and preparations for war is the refusal to pay portions of the income tax that goes to the military. Michael Robinson, rabbi of Temple Israel of Northern Westchester, in Croton-on-Hudson, New York, and his wife, Ruth Robinson, cantor and artist, take such a stand. Relating the role of civil disobedience in Jewish history from Puah and Shifra, the Hebrew midwives who refused to obey the Pharaoh and helped Hebrew male infants to survive, to Jeremiah, who opposed the policies of his government during a time of war, Rabbi Robinson articulates his beliefs that we are called to speak out and act on behalf of God and of each sacred human life. "We are to follow the State when it does not conflict with our obedience to God. When the modern pharaoh, the State, stands against life, then we must stand against the State." For Robinson, draft refusal, tax resistance, and illegal demonstration are ways of resisting on behalf of life and at the same time of fulfilling the obligations of Jewish faith. "The Talmud tells us that whoever is able to protest against the trangressions of the family and does not; whoever is able to protest against the transgressions of the community and does not; whoever is able to protest against the transgressions of the entire world and does not, that person is held responsible for the transgressions of the family, the community, and the entire world. We must speak out with our words, our lives, our actions."[24]

The Robinsons' refusal to pay the forty percent of their income tax that goes for military spending illustrates their Jewish commitment. In their letter to the Internal Revenue Service in 1982, the Robinsons claim conscientious objection on the basis of religious conviction.

We refuse to contribute to death and destruction. We give our energy, our efforts and our resources to the work of peace. We believe in the commandment "Thou shalt not kill." We wish to do harm to no other human beings but seek only "to love our neighbors as ourselves." We believe that every human being, created in the image of God, is a sacred life. We cannot contribute to the destruction of a single life. We seek to heal, not to hurt. We do not believe that the military budget is good for children, that it enhances human life. Ever more terrifying weapons of destruction threaten the very existence of life on earth. We cannot in conscience pay taxes which will pay for the building and maintenance of weapons of death and destruction. . . . We are people of Faith. We cannot pray for peace and pay for war.[25]

On May 30, 1985, a dozen Jews marched near the South African Embassy in Washington, D.C., to protest apartheid. Lucy Steinitz, executive director of The Jewish Family and Children's Service of Baltimore, issued the following statement before her arrest:

I am here as a Jew, as a child of Holocaust survivors, and as a human being—as someone who identifies with oppressed Blacks and other non-whites in South Africa. Based on the personal history and value of my own family and of my people—the Jewish people—I am here because I understand the enormously important role that others (outsiders) play—that is, people who are not currently oppressed, you and me. We are standing up to be counted, we are offering support, giving up comforts, and taking risks—however small—to act in solidarity against the governmental forces in South Africa. This is what Judaism teaches us all: to actively pursue justice on behalf of the dignity of each human soul. This is also what Bishop Desmond Tutu asked of Americans when he visited here. This solidarity is the lifeblood that sustains imprisoned, enslaved, and oppressed peoples wherever they are.[26]

A BURGEONING FEMINIST CONSCIOUSNESS

A third movement within contemporary Jewish life is the burgeoning feminist consciousness. Feminism is active within all three branches of Judaism—Orthodox, Conservative and Reform—and is extremely strong among secular Jewish women. Citing the patriarchal quality of past and present Judaism as the fundamental issue, proponents call for dealing directly with this most basic injustice. Many positions are encompassed within this critique, from simply a call for changes in leadership patterns to substantive criticism of a tradition formed for and around men.[27]

To translate these views into reality is, of course, difficult within the patriarchal mainstream of Jewish religiosity and institutional life. The founding of *Lilith* magazine in 1976 was one such step, and soon the *Lilith* office became a national clearing house for the growing Jewish women's movement. Susan Weidman Schneider, editor of the magazine, recalls that "queries came in every day from women wanting guidance on their path toward integrating feminism and Judaism. Information was needed on how to find speakers for conferences, women serving as rabbis, nonsexist Jewish day care, topics for a dissertation on Jewish women's history, women's groups dealing with midlife crisis, religious support for abortion rights, and much, much more."[28]

Since 1976, many Jewish feminist groups have come into being to help Jewish women address a variety of concerns. One such concern is battered Jewish women, a reality the Jewish community is reluctant to face. Responding to the issue, Jewish feminists have organized shelters for battered women in New York, Washington, D.C., and Tel Aviv. They schedule conferences, write articles and books, and continue to inform the Jewish community of the urgency and horror of domestic violence. Other issues include child care, abortion rights, equitable divorce and the need for increased employment opportunities.[29]

Another concern is retrieving and creating Jewish ritual that honors and helps empower women. At least two rituals are important here: *Rosh Chodesh*, the celebration of the new moon, and *Brit B'not Yisrael,* the entry of an infant girl into the covenant of the daughters of Israel.

Most of the calendar celebrations in Judaism are holidays in which men traditionally perform most of the ritual and women serve as handmaidens, performing such functions as preparing the meals and cleaning the home. An exception is *Rosh Chodesh*, the first day of the month, which, because the Hebrew calendar is a lunar one, falls at the new moon. The relative neglect of this ancient holiday is being corrected among contemporary feminists. For example, legends based on the Talmudic story of creation say that the smaller moon will one day be restored to equality with the sun; feminists "draw parallels between the moon's future equality with the sun and the equality of women that is to come." At the same time, women celebrate the connection of their bodily rhythms with those of the universe. An example of the *Rosh Chodesh* ceremony occurred at a luncheon meeting of a Task Force on the Role of the Jewish Woman in a Changing Society, sponsored by the New York Federation of Jewish Philanthropies. As Susan Weidman Schneider reports, Arlene Agus gave a *dvar Torah* (short instructive talk on Jewish law) and its significance, and all the food served was round (quiche, pies), signifying fertility and femaleness. "It's a tradition to eat round food and new fruits at *Rosh Chodesh*, to refrain from your usual work on at least half of the day of the new moon, and to incorporate certain practices into the celebration itself. These include giving charity *(tzedakah),* which on this occasion might appropriately be earmarked for women's causes or projects; lighting a candle or candles (a candle floating in a dish of water is especially lovely and moonlike); a feast featuring at least some round foods and the recital of special prayers for the new month. A study session or discussion on the holidays or themes of the month ahead might follow."[30]

Welcoming a Jewish daughter into the world has taken second place to welcoming a Jewish son. The *brit milah,* or circumcision, is central to welcoming the male infant, and not surprisingly the main participants are male. Increasingly, however, a ceremony of welcome for the female infant is being adopted. It includes prayers, wishes and dreams for the child as she grows in her womanhood and in her Judaism. Emphasized with a new sense of pride and empowerment are her biblical foremothers. Aviva Cantor created a prayer for the birth ceremony of Yael Deborah.

We wish Yael inspiration from the examples of our foremothers: from Lilith swift and unequivocal resistance to tyranny and the fortitude to face the consequences; from Eve (Chava) the hope to choose life and sustain it after Paradise was lost; from Noah's wife the nurturing qualities and patience to be a steward for Earth's creatures; from Sarah the faith to follow a dream into wilderness and to believe the impossible is possible; from Rebecca (Rivka) the wisdom to overcome the dead hand of custom; from Leah endurance and perseverance in the face of loneliness; from Rachel the compassion and love for her sister that spared Leah pain and anguish; from Dina the ability to take risks to break out of confinement (break barriers) to seek friendship with other women; from midwives Shifrah and Puah the courage to defy death to rescue the next generation; from Miriam the ability to be outspoken in her views even when they were unpopular; from Deborah (Dvora) the self-esteem that enabled her to rally and lead resistance and to take pride in her achievements; from Ya'el, whose name she carries, the courage to do what she knew she had to do. From all these, our foremothers whose actions were recorded in our Torah, and from the countless others in our history both known and unknown to us, may Yael seek and draw insight, inspiration and support.[31]

The incorporation of feminism into Jewish life is critical for the entire Jewish community. As Dr. Paula Hyman, Dean of the College of Jewish Studies of the Jewish Theological Seminary, states, the commitment to feminist issues challenges the very survival of Judaism. "If the subordination of women is at the core of Judaism, then Judaism doesn't deserve to survive. As a feminist, I am not willing to accept my subordination and the subordination of my daughters and my sisters as the price for the survival of Jewish tradition. We are, in a sense, calling Judaism morally to account—Judaism is on trial in some ways for us. It must be able to contend with this moral issue—and resolve it."[32]

These three movements of renewal represent a small but growing minority seeking a redirection of Jewish life. In one sense, they all pose the same question: What does it mean to be faithful to the Jewish community and to the world? Though answers vary, a commonality is seen in their thrust for inclusivity (e.g., religious and secular Jews, women and men), their search for a renewal of community life in the midst of Holocaust and empowerment, and their refusal to be silent despite the pressure from political and religious neoconservatives for a moratorium on critique of the Jewish community.

And yet they remain a distinct minority in the Jewish community. The theological voice of Arthur Waskow, which attempts to posit Jewish language and symbol as the coherent center of the Jewish people, strikes many as too "religious" after the Holocaust. On the other hand, civil disobedience, especially relating to the military, is often seen as a threatening gesture to an America viewed as a haven for a persecuted people and as a support for an embattled Israel. A religious Zionism which speaks of Palestinians as brothers and sisters fights an increasingly difficult struggle in Israel and in the United States, where Palestinians are labeled and dismissed as terrorists. Feminism in the religious sphere is either quietly integrated into mainstream Judaism or rejected outright, but the radical critique and tranformation it proposes is ignored.

Thus the third era of Jewish history as announced by Irving Greenberg is more complicated than one might have expected. It is filled with competing voices and values, each with its own insights and limitation. The third era began with the Holocaust and the need for empowerment; now within empowerment in the United States and Israel we confront the possibility of exile and renewal. What emerged from the Holocaust was a shattered witness; today our empowerment is haunted by the possibility of betrayal.

CHAPTER 4

Liberation Struggles and the Jewish Community

It is perhaps an oddity of history that the Exodus and the prophetic stories the Jewish people formed and bequeathed to the world are being taken seriously by contemporary Christians in a way that is increasingly difficult for the Jewish community to understand. As the Jewish people learn more and more about the trappings of power, a prophetic Christianity is emerging from powerless Christians of Latin America, Africa, Asia, and North America.

Rooted in impoverished communities and inspired by the gospel proclamation of justice and peace, a new understanding of Christianity has emerged, one that adopts a preferential option for the poor and advocates liberation from oppressive social structures. The recently empowered contemporary Jewish community, however, appears fearful—and perhaps threatened—by such a prophetic revival within Christianity, for, in its use of the Exodus and the prophets, Christian liberation theology speaks for those on the underside of history, the marginalized and the oppressed. Could not the Jewish tradition, which is atrophying under the mantle of political empowerment, benefit from a sympathetic dialogue with this movement? Might not such a dialogue enhance our understanding not only of those struggling under oppression but also of our own history? Since oppression characterizes much of our own story, could we not in solidarity add the depth of our struggle to those who struggle today?

66

The revival of the Exodus and prophetic traditions in the Christian theologies of liberation is itself heir to a long history of interpreting the Exodus within political movements. As Michael Walzer, a Jewish political thinker, demonstrates in his study of the Exodus in Western history, reference to the Exodus in protest and radical movements is so common that its absence is the exception. It figures prominently in such diverse settings as the political argument of the radical monk Savonarola, who preached twenty-two sermons on the Book of Exodus in the months before his execution; the self-understanding of the English Puritans on their "errand into the wilderness"; and the writings of the early socialist Moses Hess.[1]

Much of the theoretical grounding for this Christian renewal is expressed in Black, Latin American, and Asian liberation theologies. A brief review of representative figures of these movements helps illustrate the revival of these themes from the Hebrew Scriptures.

BLACK LIBERATION THEOLOGY

When James Cone, the first person to articulate a theological component of the Black Power movement, searched for a definition of a Christianity which supported the *"complete emancipation of black people from white oppression by whatever means black people deem necessary,"* he found little support in the otherworldly Jesus of white European and North American Christianity. Theologians who analyzed the idea of God's righteousness were far removed from the exigencies of daily life. This had the effect of supporting a racist society where "people suffer and die for lack of political justice." A Black theologian has a task far beyond theological disputation and speculation. As Cone articulates in his groundbreaking 1969 book, *Black Theology and Black Power,* a Black theologian wants to know what the gospel has to say to a person who cannot get work to support his or her family because the society is unjust. "He wants to know what is God's Word to the countless black boys and girls who are fatherless and motherless because white society decreed that blacks have no rights. Unless there is a word from Christ to the helpless, then why should they respond to him? How do we relate the gospel of Christ to people whose daily existence is one of hunger or even worse, despair? Or do we simply refer them to the next world?"[2]

For Cone the answer is found in the biblical concept of the righteousness of God. This concept refers less to abstract speculation about the quality of God's being that is commonly found in Greek philosophy than to God's activity in human history, in God's desire for the oppressed to be free.

> Israel as a people initially came to know God through the Exodus. It was Yahweh who emancipated her from Egyptian bondage and subsequently established a covenant with her at Sinai, promising: "You have seen what I did to the Egyptians, and how I bore you on eagles' wings and brought you to myself. Now therefore, if you will obey my voice and keep my covenant, you shall be my own possession among all peoples. . . . You shall be to me a kingdom of priests and a holy nation" (Exod. 19:4–6). Divine righteousness means that God will be faithful to his promise, that his purposes for Israel will not be thwarted. Israel, therefore, need not worry about her weakness and powerlessness in a world of mighty military powers, "for all the earth is mine" (Exod. 19:5). The righteousness of God means that he will protect her from the ungodly menacing of other nations. Righteousness means God is doing justice, that he is putting right what men have made wrong.[3]

Cone's exploration of the Jewish Scriptures provides a key to the understanding of his people's history and of contemporary hopes for liberation. His book *The Spirituals and the Blues* demonstrates that the central theological concept in the Black spirituals is the divine liberation of the oppressed from slavery. According to Cone, the spirituals show that Black slaves believed that God did not create Africans to be slaves and that slavery was in fact "irreconcilable with their African past and their knowledge of the Christian gospel." Instead they portray a God who is involved in the history of a struggling people: the deliverance of the children of Israel from bondage in Egypt is also the story of deliverance of an African people enslaved in America.

O freedom ! O freedom!
O freedom over me!
An' befo' I'd be a slave,
I'll be buried in my grave,
An' go home to my Lord an' be free.

My Lord delivered Daniel,
Why can't he deliver me?

When Israel was in Egypt's land,
Let my people go;
Oppressed so hard they could not stand,
Let my people go;
Go down, Moses, 'way down in Egypt's land;
Tell ole Pharaoh
Let my people go.[4]

The critical task of a Black theology of liberation is to break through the status-quo-reinforcing Christianity held by white America. Cone is energized by the fact that his insights are grounded in the expressions of the history of his people. But for Christians the ultimate foundation is the life and meaning of Jesus Christ, and often Jesus is seen as otherworldly, divorced from the political realm. Cone addresses this issue by placing Jesus in continuity with the Jewish Exodus and prophetic traditions. For Cone the central theme of the Jewish Scriptures, involvement in history and the liberation of the people, is the key to understanding Jesus. Jesus' reading of the Isaiahan prophecies of messianic justice in the Nazareth synagogue represents for Cone the scandal that the "gospel means liberation, that this liberation comes to the poor, and that it gives them the strength and courage to break the conditions of servitude." This is the meaning of incarnation: "God in Christ comes to the weak and the helpless, and becomes one with them, taking their condition of oppression as his own and thus transforming their slave-existence into a liberated existence." Incarnation is followed by death and resurrection, and for Cone, Jesus' earthly life achieves a radical significance not possible without that death and resurrection. The cross and resurrection mean that Jesus' ministry with the poor "was God himself effecting his will to liberate the oppressed. The Jesus story is the poor person's story, because God in Christ becomes poor and weak in order that the oppressed might become liberated from poverty and powerlessness. God becomes the victim in their place and thus transforms the condition of slavery into the battle ground for the struggle of freedom." This is what the resurrection of Jesus means: "The oppressed are freed for struggle, for battle in the pursuit of humanity."[5]

Thus Cone not only places Jesus in continuity with the Jewish Scriptures; he places Jesus in the dynamic of the Exodus and the prophets, a dynamic which brings the message of liberation to the fore. The genius of Cone's theology, like that of his struggling ancestors, is that he rarely mentions Jesus alone but rather in the company of Moses, sent by the God of the Exodus and of the prophets.

LATIN AMERICAN LIBERATION THEOLOGY

At the same time as Cone was thinking through the theological dimensions of Black Power in the United States, the struggle for justice in Latin America was developing a theological voice. At the Second General Conference of Latin American Bishops at Medellín, Colombia, in August-September 1968, the situation of Latin America was described as one of injustice and despair that "cried to the heavens." The Exodus paradigm was invoked.

Just as Israel of old, the first People (of God), felt the saving presence of God when He delivered them from the oppression of Egypt by the passage through the sea and led them to the promised land, so we also, the new People of God, cannot cease to feel his saving passage in view of true development, which is the passage for each and all, from conditions of life that are less human, to those that are more human. *Less human:* the material needs of those who are deprived of the minimum living conditions, and the moral needs of those who are mutilated by selfishness. *Less human:* the oppressive structures that come from the abuse of ownership and of power and from exploitation of workers or from unjust

transactions. *More human:* overcoming misery by the possession of necessities; victory over social calamities; broadening
of knowledge; the acquisition of cultural advantages. *More
human also:* an increase in respect for the dignity of others;
orientation toward the spirit of poverty; cooperation for the
common good; the will for peace. *More human still:* ac-
knowledgement, on man's part, of the supreme values and of
God who is their source and term. *More human, finally,* and
especially, faith, the gift of God, accepted by men of good
will and unity in the charity of Christ, who calls us all to
participation, as sons, in the life of the living God who is the
father of all men.[6]

Three years later, in 1971, Gustavo Gutiérrez, a Peruvian priest
and theologian, published his seminal work *Teología de la libera-
ción, Perspectivas.* The English translation, *A Theology of Liberation: History, Politics and Salvation* appeared in 1973. Central to
Gutiérrez's thesis is that faith in God is intimately linked with works
in behalf of justice. In fact, God is a liberating God who acts in
behalf of struggling peoples and encourages them to act in their
own behalf as well. According to Gutiérrez, biblical faith is "faith
in a God who reveals himself through historical events, a God who
saves in history," and the Exodus is the prime example of such
historical activity.[7]

The liberation of Israel is a political action. It is the breaking
away from a situation of despoliation and misery and the
beginning of the construction of a just and fraternal society.
It is the suppression of disorder and the creation of a new
order. The initial chapters of Exodus describe the oppression
in which the Jewish people lived in Egypt, in that "land of
slavery" (13:3; 20:2; Deut. 5:6): repression (1:10–11), alienated work (5:6–14), humiliations (1:13–14), enforced birth
control policy (1:15–22). Yahweh then awakens the vocation
of a liberator: Moses. "I have indeed seen the misery of my
people in Egypt. I have heard their outcry against their slave-
masters. I have taken heed of their sufferings, and have come
down to rescue them from the power of Egypt. . . . I have
seen the brutality of the Egyptians towards them. Come now;

I will send you to Pharaoh and you shall bring my people
Israel out of Egypt." (3:7–10)[8]

Like Cone, Gutiérrez sees the Exodus event as paradigmatic for the
present. "It remains vital and contemporary due to similar historical experiences which the people of God undergo."[9]

It is within the dynamic of the Exodus and the prophets that the
historical Jesus can be recovered in his political dimensions. In the
discourse, Gutiérrez sees Jesus as a person who confronted the
established political and religious powers of his day. As he criticized
inauthentic religion he proclaimed his opposition to the rich and
powerful as a radical option for the poor. Jesus' trial was a political
one: "Jesus died at the hands of the political authorities, the
oppressors of the Jewish people." Though Jesus did not place
himself within any one political faction, the gospel stories point to a
deeper political reality. For Gutiérrez, the life and preaching of
Jesus postulate the search for a new kind of person in a qualitatively different society. Although the kingdom must not be confused with the establishment of a just society, this does not mean, in
Gutiérrez's mind, that the kingdom is indifferent to this society.
Instead, "The announcement of the kingdom reveals to society
itself the aspiration for a just society and leads it to discover
unsuspected dimensions and unexplored paths. The kingdom is
realized in a society of brotherhood and justice." It is this realization that opens up the promise and hope of complete communion
of all persons with God.[10]

ASIAN LIBERATION THEOLOGY

As Christians throughout Asia are exploring liberation themes,
Korean Christians are finding the Hebrew Scriptures important to
their own identity and crucial to the development of minjung
theology. "Minjung" is a Korean word combining two Chinese
characters: "min," translated as "people," and "jung," translated
as "the mass." Thus "minjung" means "the mass of the people," or
"mass," or simply "the people." As the Korean theologian Suh
Kwang-Sun David describes it, minjung theology grew from the
experience of the people laboring under an unjust political regime
and thus contains a socio-political biography of oppressed Korean
Christians. "Theology of minjung is a creation of those Christians
who were forced to reflect upon their Christian discipleship in

basement interrogation rooms, in trials, facing court-martial tribunals, hearing the allegation of prosecutors, and in making their own final defense. They reflected on their Christian commitment in prison cells, in their letters from prison to families and friends, in their readings of books sent by friends all over the world, in their unemployment, in their stay at home under house arrest, while subject to a twenty-four-hour watch over their activities, and during visits with their friends." Out of that suffering and struggling, Korean Christians want to speak of what they have learned and reflected upon theologically, and to share this with others who in their own social and political context are searching for a relevant theology in Asia.[11]

Though in the Jewish Scriptures there is no exact parallel for the term minjung, scholars have searched the experience of the early Hebrews and have found similarities. Moon Hee-Suk Cyris begins an extended analysis of the similarities between the Exodus tradition and the minjung by showing that in essence the Jewish Scriptures are the history of belief about the minjung's liberation movement as well as a creedal statement about their original status as bearers of the image of God in the creation narrative in Genesis. When later the minjung are economically under the dominion of the upper class and the powerful, the Jewish Scriptures describe the minjung subjectively, calling them the people of God and thus making them the subjects of history. Therefore, the meaning of minjung in their relation to God and their welfare becomes God's concern. Cyris's conclusion is that the minjung of today are in the midst of an Exodus/prophets paradigm and that the three characteristics of Moses, Amos, and Micah—that is, living and identifying with the people, becoming advocates for the oppressed, and remaining commoners rather than professional prophets—are relevant today. "Like Moses, Amos, and Micah, we in Korea must resolve to follow the footsteps of the true prophet living among our oppressed people and standing against political, social, and economic oppression. To work for the transformation of our society is to participate in the task of ushering in the Kingdom of God."[12]

JEWISH RESPONSES

The reactions of the Jewish community to the emergence of liberation theology, as intimated earlier, have been diverse, from ignorance to curiosity to critique and dismissal. To the curious, liberation theology represents the possibility of a politically active force for uplifting poor and oppressed people, though for the curious, their knowledge of Christianity (and of Judaism too) is often limited, and thus they observe from a distance. For Jewish theologians and institutional leaders, the rise of liberation theology can be more difficult: some see this revival as an ancient form of Christian triumphalism returning in a new guise. At the same time, for many Jews liberation theology's call for societal transformation presages chaos; they fear such restructuring can lead only to totalitarian Marxist regimes.[13]

There is another element here as well. In most liberation theologies the Jewish Exodus is used as a paradigm of revolution, but contemporary Jews are nowhere to be found in the writings of the theologians. This continues an age-old Christian tradition of seeing the Jewish people as bequeathing the "Old Testament" and Jesus and then disappearing from history, their mission accomplished. The use of the Jewish story is coupled with our historical invisibility. Thus, liberation theologians often miss an element crucial to the Exodus story itself: that it has a history of interpretation by the people who lived the story and who live today.[14]

The movement to place Jesus within the history of the Jewish people—which is at the same time the rescuing of Jesus from various Christian traditions' otherworldliness—also opens once again the horrible landscape of the crucifixion. For Jews, of course, the accusation of responsibility for crucifying Jesus is an indelible mark of the last 1900 years—years which culminated in the death camps of the Nazi period. And since that time, ecumenical relations have been predicated on the removal of that stigma, which to some extent has been accomplished since Vatican II. But some liberation theologians in their description of the historical Jesus come dangerously close to posing this problem again. This, combined with a militant Christian social movement, understandably arouses Jewish concern. The sign of the cross as a banner for social reform is greeted with both skepticism and fear.[15]

Moreover, the ecumenical movement over the last thirty years has primarily taken place among educated white middle- and upper middle-class Christians and Jews who have vested interests in continuing the political status quo. The rise of liberation theology questions the religious integrity of these Christians who base their faith on cultural symbols and ritual assent rather than on socio-political transformation. Have Jews been talking with people whose Christianity is now being challenged? The ironic twist is that despite the Holocaust, many Jews are now quite comfortable with the institutional Church. Moreover, they are extremely uneasy with grass-roots Christian movements. This comfort is bound up with preferring known religious affirmations to the unknown, but also with the institutional protection sometimes afforded the Jewish community by Catholic and Protestant institutions that have moral and political leverage in Western societies. That some unfamiliar configuration of Christianity and Christian institutions might emerge raises the level of Jewish anxiety.

The most frightening aspect for parts of the Jewish community, however, is the Third World character of liberation theology and its emerging cross-cultural solidarity. Charges of imperialism and neo-colonialism are part and parcel of these movements, and the United States is a frequent target in their critique. At the same time, Israel is heavily involved on the side of the government in some of the areas where liberation struggles are the strongest and most sym-bolic, as noted earlier. Thus the fear that movements of liberation will not only be critical of America but also of Israel leads some to accuse these movements of anti-Semitism.

In a more significant way, the theological reflections of the Jewish community after the Holocaust do not resonate with trium-phal language in the theological realm. On the one hand, the Exodus—God who rescues the people from bondage—is contra-dicted by the Holocaust event; on the other hand, the need for empowerment renders prophetic voices naive and even dangerous. If Christians have appropriated the Jewish Exodus and the proph-ets without reference to the contemporary heirs of the Hebrew Scriptures, it is also true that the Jewish community, because of our history, has been reluctant to claim its own heritage.

It is clear, then, that the impasse between the Christian theologies of liberation and the Jewish community is multifaceted and com-plex, with many strains and tensions that will exist into the future. The question, it seems, is not how to go beyond the tension but how to move constructively within it. The choice to be with and for the empire in this struggle seems, on the face of it, to be safer and less complex: to choose to move with those who seek community is to promote a configuration that may change both the Christian and the Jewish perception of the world and of ourselves. By placing ourselves in the struggle for justice, we of the Jewish community may discover the other side of our own history.

At the outset it seems that the theological task of dialogue between the post-Holocaust Jewish community and the emerging theologies of liberation is framed in confrontation: a God unable to rescue the people within the Holocaust versus a God leading the people to freedom and justice. Or, if Israel is a redemptive sign somehow connected to God, the connection remains hidden while the Christian theologians of liberation boldly announce the building of God's kingdom. And yet, when analyzed more closely, the triumphal strain in liberation theology is increasingly countered by strains of doubt in religious language. For the liberation of the oppressed, like the experience of the concentration camps, is not a superficial testimony to religious certainty. Rather it is a test of God's fidelity and of human struggle characterized by abandonment and death.

To those in the struggle for liberation, theological language is increasingly found wanting. Joan Casañas, a Spaniard and long-time resident of Chile, describes the gap between revolutionary activity and theological language in a fascinating essay, "The Task of Making God Exist." Casañas begins with the question "Activist, What Do You See in the Night?" and cites a conversation with Christian activists after the overthrow of Salvador Allende's government in 1973, shortly before the massacre of the Chilean people began.

We were discussing the importance of the religious language and expressions of Christian faith that Chileans, the majority of whom were believers, were incorporating into the struggle that was then underway in their homeland. We reached this conclusion: there is no need to tell the people that God is with them, that God will help them to overcome the right-wing plot; that God is their friend and will save them. For the more a people becomes organized and fights for socialism, the more it realizes that no one outside its world, not even God, is doing anything on behalf of the people's liberation other than what the people itself is doing. It would be better for us to be silent about what God is and what God can do.[16]

The problem is that most theologians, even liberation theologians, want to mold the experience of those who struggle for justice into theological categories to which the people themselves no longer relate. But activists want to know "what we are living through and seeing, and what has been given to us in the present; not what we have been 'taught' as being 'good,' and what we have 'assented to' with 'religious' fidelity." For Casañas, a concrete example of this is the prayer of petition.[17]

Many individuals and groups of proven praxis in revolutionary faith, and with obvious practical love for the oppressed lived in openness to the transcendence proposed by the gospel, do not feel comfortable with a prayer that consists in asking for things from God, even though those things may be justice or the strength to fight for it. . . . A little old woman from the Christian community in my neighborhood, a working woman who had been exploited all her life and who was very much aware of the nature of the conflict in our society, remarked at a community faith celebration, "Yes, we have asked God often to let justice come and let Somoza go, but God does not listen at all." I think this checks, or even checkmates, the most brilliant pages of theology, as far as talk about God and God's treatment of us is concerned. Hers was not the sarcasm of the rationalist spinning theories about God, but the disappointment of the poor exploited person who has nothing against God, but who senses that God should be something other than what has generally been thought and taught.[18]

At the same time that Casañas rejects talk of God's omnipotence, he also rejects the more recent theories of the crucified God who refuses to act with force and instead suffers with the people until liberation. The reason for the rejection of this theological category is similar to the prayer of petition: revolutionary activists do not see this kind of God in the night.[19]

For Casañas, direct knowledge of God is impossible, especially in an unjust society. Those who affirm God's presence in an unjust society often see God as legitimator of that injustice—but can that conception of God be accepted? Theism becomes a form of idolatry, a worship of false gods. In this case a certain atheism is necessary, a refusal to believe in a God who sanctions oppression. Still, the theologians who recognize most theism as idolatrous continue to place limitations on those who explore God through revolutionary activity.

> When those who fight and die today for real, concrete justice—the justice that capitalism impedes—do not speak of God and, for example, do not experience God as Father, it is thought and said, even in the most "advanced" theology or pastoral writing, that something is lacking in them. It is said that they must be "evangelized," that we have a "message" to give them, that we know something about God that they do not know. It seems to me that we are involving ourselves in a serious contradiction between knowledge acquired through conscious practice and knowledge acquired through learned and religiously accepted truths. . . . If many of those fighting and dying selflessly for the people's liberation (that is, placed in the practical life-situation acknowledged to be optimal for "knowing God") have not discovered that "God exists" and is "Father," is it not possible that this "message" that "God exists" and is "Father" may not be as profound, at least in its formulation, as it has generally seemed to us? Has what many activists have not discovered by giving their lives for the oppressed been discovered by a Videla, a Pinochet, a Somoza, or the bishops who honor them? Has some "apostle" told it to them, and they believed it with all their mind and heart? Is it so easy to know something about God in a world where injustice is so rampant?[20]

What Casañas is describing is a new understanding of fidelity, a broadening of language and conceptualization in the struggle for justice. Under such conditions the certainty of God falls away, though the absolute refusal of God is also questioned. For some, religious tradition does nothing but hinder the revolutionary struggle; others admire its continuity among the people as a source of strength in adversity; still others see tradition as providing clues to a possible reconstruction. Casañas' point is that those who struggle in the present proceed with the insights that are bequeathed within the moment, and that entering the depths of history is the way of fidelity.

> There is the Colombian guerrilla fighter who often prays the rosary with some of his comrades. And there is the guerrilla fighter who rejects all sentiments of a religious nature, or even an openness to transcendence, because of the great fear he has of succumbing to rapture that would curtail his involvement in the struggle. And there is the one who seems cold and insensitive to anything that might be a symbol, or poetry, or a mystique, but who readily and sincerely adapts to whatever the circumstances require for liberating efficacy. And there is the Montonero leader who, after years in jail and exile, attended a Mass on the fourth anniversary of the assassination of Miguel Enríquez and stated publicly that the fact that he, the Montonero, was able to escape from jail and from Argentina was "a gift from God" (and no one dared ask him what the death of Miguel Enríquez was, on the part of God). There was another one, who did not attend that Mass, because for tactical reasons he feared his presence would be interpreted as a compromise with the religious language and symbolism that, for him, mask a kind of magic. And there was the one who attended for the sake of solidarity, observed, listened, and departed, saying that all this was not so bad, that there was something authentic about it, but that it had been expressed better by the "unbelieving" relatives and political leaders who had spoken at the Mass than by the priests with all their homilies and prayers.[21]

As Casañas moves from a triumphal Christianity to one which is open to the insights which come from struggle and death, the Jewish experience of the Holocaust comes into view. Though faith did not disappear in the Holocaust, certainty did and the Exodus and prophetic traditions are confronted with a horror which shatters ancient precepts and beliefs. If Casañas starts with the question "Activist, what do you see in the night?", the Holocaust raises a similar question for the Jewish victims: "What did you see in the night?" Is it possible that by recounting the night vision of the Holocaust victims we might be able to provide the basis for a dialogue with those who today are peering into the darkness with fear and trepidation? Could it be that we are not alone in the night but are joined by sisters and brothers in a new continuity of struggle and affirmation, a retrospective solidarity across religious and geographic boundaries which might portend a flesh and blood solidarity for the future? As we probe the night together, perhaps we can begin to imagine a broader tradition of faith and struggle which is confessional for past atrocities, is bold in allowing the experiences of peoples to speak, unfettered by religious or political constraints, in short, one that allows the reality of night to speak.[22]

As with the night of which Casañas speaks, the night of Holocaust is ever present. The darkness contains many peoples. They are different—each with their own history and voice; they are also similar—pertaining to oppression and resistance, abandonment and affirmation, prayer and negation. But in the night, if just for a moment, they are one.

Consider the reality of death and abandonment first from a Jewish mother of Eastern Europe, then from the eyes of a pastoral worker in Guatemala.

When I came up to the place we saw people naked lined up. But we were still hoping that this was only torture. Maybe there is hope—hope of living. . . . One could not leave the line, but I wished to see—what are they doing on the hillock? Is there anyone down below? I turned my head and saw that some three or four rows were already killed on the ground. There were some twelve people amongst the dead. I also want to mention what my child said while we were lined up in the Ghetto, she said, "Mother, why did you make me wear the Shabbat dress; we are going to be shot," and when we stood near the dug-outs, near the grave, she said, "Mother, why are we waiting, let us run!" Some of the young people tried to run, but they were caught immediately, and they were shot right there.

I had my daughter in my arms and ran after the truck. There were mothers who had two or three children and held them in their arms running after the truck. We ran all the way. There were those who fell—we were not allowed to help them rise. They were shot right there wherever they fell. . . . When we all reached the destination, the people from the truck were already down and they were undressed—all lined up. All my family was there—undressed, lined up. The people from the truck, those who arrived before us. . . . When it came to our turn, our father was beaten. We prayed, we begged with my father to undress, but he would not undress, he wanted to keep his underclothes. He did not want to stand naked. Then they tore off the clothing of the old man and he was shot. I saw it with my own eyes. And then they took my mother, and she said, let us go before her; but they caught mother and shot her too; and then there was my grandmother, my father's mother standing there; she was eighty years old and she had two children in her arms. And then there was my father's sister. She also had children in her arms and she was shot on the spot with the babies in her arms. . . .[23]

All day long we were fleeing. We ran seeking the ravines. We brought all the injured from the other villages; there were many. The largest number were women and little children. We hid in the mountains, but the women wore clothes of many colors, and from the helicopters they could see us very well. We saw the helicopters begin to fly in circles, surrounding us all. They began to machine-gun the people. The only way of saving ourselves was to run to the ravine and throw ourselves into it, which was quite steep. We began to run and run to the mountain, falling and falling. The small children ran alone. They were being left behind, getting lost among so many people; and all shouted, "Mama, Mama." One woman cried; she cried a lot, talking in the language of Quiche. I didn't understand well what she said. Someone said to me, "She's crying because her child was killed." I had seen the little child. She had been born 15 days earlier. The woman had carried the child on her back. She fell when she was running, and she fell on the child and it was killed. She said, "God is going to punish me. I have a great sin on me because I have killed my child." A woman said, "God is not with us, God has abandoned us. If we haven't done anything bad, if we haven't asked for so much, why does God abandon us now?"[24]

Commonality can be found in resistance as well. During the Somoza dictatorship two Nicaraguan peasants discuss their movement toward armed resistance, as does a Warsaw ghetto fighter.

ALEJANDRO: "One sentence here is very clear: 'Therefore do not fear the people.' The fear you have is that they're going to do you some harm. And when are they going to do you harm? When you're against certain systems, certain injustices. That is, we're absolutely forbidden to be afraid of telling the truth, of being against anything that will endanger us, even our lives. It's clear that for the sake of justice we have to risk even our bodies. They can kill the body but they can't kill the cause for which we fight. And it spreads even wider: The Gospel tells us some words here in secret that we're supposed to shout."

Another boy said: "I think like you, Alejandro, that here, the government we have in Nicaragua, it does whatever it wants with us, with the people, and because we're afraid we don't fight against these injustices. According to what it says here we shouldn't be afraid of that, because if they're doing an injustice to the people we should fight. And all right, let's die, the body isn't worth anything and they can destroy our bodies but not our souls. It seems to me then that we ought to fight and not submit."[25]

The Warsaw ghetto fighter writes:

The number of our losses, that is, the victims killed by shooting and by the fires, in which men, women and children have been consumed, is immense. Our last days are approaching. But so long as we have arms in our hands we will continue to fight and resist. We have rejected the German ultimatum demanding our capitulation. Aware that our day is at hand, we demand from you to remember how we were betrayed. What we have experienced cannot be described in words. We are aware of one thing only: what has happened has exceeded all our dreams. The Germans twice ran from the ghetto . . . I have the feeling that great things are happening, that what we have dared is of great importance. Beginning with this evening we are passing to partisan tactics. . . . Keep well, my dear. Perhaps we shall meet again. But what really matters is that the dream of my life has come true. Jewish self-defense in the Warsaw Ghetto has become a fact. Jewish armed resistance and retaliation have become a reality. I have been the witness of the magnificent heroic struggle of our Jewish fighters.[26]

Prayer becomes an act of affirmation, a prelude to martyrdom. As told by an eyewitness, Shlomo Zlichovsky, a Polish Jew and a teacher, prepared for his death in much the same way as did Salvadoran Archbishop Oscar Romero.

Then, as the last preparations were being made for the hanging, I, too, looked into the face of Shlomo Zlichovsky. It was smiling with joy. I stood in the crowded place, in the midst of many humiliated Jews. But suddenly a spirit of encouragement passed over all of us. The gallows were standing in a row, under each of them a chair in readiness. The Germans were in no hurry. A pity to waste a single moment of the "entertainment." But Shlomo Zlichovsky, still singing, urged them on: "Nu!" (come on already), and jumped on the chair in order to put his head into the hanging loop. Some moments passed. We all held our breath. Deathly silence came over the market place, . . . a silence that found its redemption as Shlomo Zlichovsky's mighty voice was shattering it in his triumphant *Shema Yisra'el.* We were all elevated; we were exalted. We shouted . . . without a voice; cried . . . without tears; straightened up . . . without a movement; and called, called altogether in the innermost recesses of our souls: *Shema Yisra'el.* ("Hear, O Israel: The Lord your God, the Lord is One").[27]

Romero writes:

> My life has been threatened many times. I have to confess that, as a Christian, I don't believe in death without resurrection. If they kill me, I will rise again in the Salvadoran people. . . . If they should go so far as to carry out their threats, I want you to know that I now offer my blood to God for justice and the resurrection of El Salvador. . . . A bishop will die, but the church of God, which is the people, will never perish.[28]

The commonality found in the night does not mitigate the unique quality of historical events, nor does it encourage a superficial universalism. Entire books are written about the absolutely unique quality of the Jewish Holocaust. But is not the loss of life during the African slave trade, estimated to be in the millions, a unique event of mass death, a holocaust, as it were, of immense proportions for the African people then and now? For the Guatemalan peasant, particularly the indigenous Indian population, is not the continuing slaughter of its people and the decimation of native peoples in the Americas over the centuries, a unique holocaust event as well? And as Western Jews, have we not participated in and benefited from these holocausts? America may be seen as a haven for Jewish people, but can this be said for the Native American and the Black? Further, the present also produces a startling picture: we, as Jews, continue to benefit from a racist society in America and are building such a society in Israel. To an alarming degree we support policies in the United States and Israel that assure continued holocausts in Central America and South Africa.[29]

The role of the United States in the atrocities of Central America and in support of the apartheid regime in South Africa, historically and today, is well documented. But the Israeli role is relatively unknown in the Jewish community, though it, too, is increasingly documented. Such operations are often unannounced and covert, dictated by the needs of survival. Yet some Jews are beginning to speak and write about these policies as forms of complicity with evil and as a denigration of our own people. If we are going to learn how to see the suffering of other peoples in the night, as we so well see our own, we need to be honest about our own present contribution to that suffering. And if it is true that the language of the Exodus and the prophets rings hollow in our experience of Holocaust, can we legitimately search for a new religious language while at the same time we contribute to the suffering of others?

Victor Perera, a Sephardic Jew, who grew up in Guatemala and has lived in Israel, has written several articles detailing Israeli involvement in Guatemala since 1977. As summarized by Jane Hunter in her monthly research report, *Israeli Foreign Affairs,* Perera presents a vivid account of the suffering of the Guatemalan people: the family of four, killed with an Uzi submachine gun for inquiring after the disappeared, to the genocidal assault on the Mayan Indians, the highlands where they are concentrated "emptied" in a scorched-earth campaign to purge guerrilla "contamination." At the same time, his article details the scope of Israeli assistance to the Guatemalan regime.

- The major arms deliveries of Galil assault rifles, Arava counter-insurgency airplanes, armored cars and assorted gear that kept the military in its bloody business after the Carter Administration, hoping to bring about an easing of human rights abuses, banned military aid to Guatemala.

- The installation of the computer system which keeps track of "subversive elements" and the computer system—this one made by the major electronics firm, Tadiran, which has also brought high technology to the white minority in South Africa—which measures the usage of water, electricity and telephone, enabling the military to pinpoint and raid houses where there is a high level of activity.

- The training—for which Israel was warmly thanked on US network TV—of soldiers loyal to Gen. Efraín Ríos Montt in his overthrow of the previous military government and in his Plan Victoria 82, the infamous scorched-earth and forced-resettlement campaign to exterminate an insurgency deeply anchored in the largely Indian Guatemalan peasantry.

- The training and inspiration of Guatemalan military officers in structuring the new "model villages" which, along with mandatory civil defense patrols, are designed to exercise total control over residents. Inspired by Israeli agricultural technology and an aberrant adaptation of the social organization of the Israeli kibbutz, the model villages are to function as vertically-integrated frozen food factories. On these state-owned plantations the captive population will grow broccoli, asparagus, watermelon "and a dozen other lucrative export crops."[30]

Israel has done little better in relation to Nicaragua. After supporting the Somoza dynasty for close to thirty years, including weapons sales right up to the end of Anastasio Somoza's reign in 1979, Israel began as early as 1983 to aid the counter-revolutionaries, responsible for the death of more than 12,000 Nicaraguan citizens. Some examples follow.

- In July 1983, Pastora received 500 AK-47 rifles from Israel via Venezuela. These weapons came from a large stash Israel had captured in Lebanon in 1982.

- FDN official Edgar Chamorro Coronel said that in October 1983 his forces had received 2,000 mostly AK–47s from Israel, which he explained had come through a private arms dealer. Chamorro stressed that only one such shipment had been received.

- On July 21, 1983, Reagan Administration officials revealed that Israel had assented to an American request and had recently begun to supply arms captured in Lebanon— artillary pieces, mortar rounds, mines, hand grenades and ammunition—to Honduras.

- On April 25, 1984, US officials in Honduras confirmed that the Contras received arms from Israel, and five months later Washington officials again noted that the Contras had "received official and private aid from Israel" and other countries. *Time* reported that "Israel funnels arms to the Contras through the Honduran Army" and, according to the respected *Latin American Weekly Report,* the CIA had been footing the bill for all of the Israeli arms shipments.

• Writing in the *Washington Post,* Bob Woodward suggested that the Contras had also made their own arrangements with Israel for arms deliveries.

• The Contras also had the benefit of Israeli intelligence experts, "retired or reserve Israeli army commandos . . . hired by shadowy private firms." Recruiters in Israel were offering top dollar—$6,500 to $10,000 a month, compared to the $5,700 rate paid former Argentine military officers.[31]

By May 1985, when the United States' aid to the counter-revolutionaries began to run out, the government of Israel was increasing its support, including the addition of Israeli military advisors.[32]

The relationship between Israel and South Africa is older and even more wider-ranging: it includes cooperation in economic, military, nuclear, scientific, and academic affairs, as well as in the areas of energy, tourism, culture, sports, transportation, agriculture, and intelligence. Of all the cooperative enterprises, the military link is the most important to South Africa.[33]

Although Israel once stated that it was abiding by the 1977 United Nations embargo on arms to South Africa, by 1983 it was widely known that Israel was violating the agreement. As Jane Hunter documents, South Africa has bought Israeli weapons, including attack boats equipped with ship-to-ship missiles, patrol boats and jet fighters, radar stations, electronic fences, infiltration alarm systems, and night-vision apparatus. At the same time, South Africa made a major commitment to help finance Israeli weapons systems, including the Lavi, Israel's fighter bomber for the 1990s. Israelis have trained South Africans in everything from naval construction to counter-insurgency techniques and "observers have noted striking similarities between Israeli and South African techniques." Cooperation between Israel and South Africa in developing a nuclear capability has been known for some years and continues today.[34]

In July 1985, Shimshon Zelniker, head of social studies at the Labor Party's college, met with Nobel laureate Bishop Desmond Tutu and other Black leaders in South Africa. In an article published in the *Jerusalem Post,* Zelniker reported that the Black leaders had "lambasted" Israel's collaboration with the white minority regime, and they spoke of similarities between South African apartheid and the plight of the Palestinians on the West Bank and Gaza. Bishop Tutu wondered how Jews could seek a monopoly of the Holocaust and at the same time refuse to understand the fascist nature of apartheid.[35]

It is important to understand the massive shift in Jewish perspective that Bishop Tutu suggests in noting Israel's support of the apartheid regime, and it is true for the cases in Guatemala and Nicaragua cited earlier, though unfortunately this hardly exhausts Israel's foreign policies worthy of mention in this regard. The three major reasons for such policies relate to economics, defense, and the increasing surrogate role for United States interests—no doubt a reasonable return payment for massive United States aid to Israel, now approaching four billion dollars a year. Yet mention survival as a reason for supporting Hitler during World War II, or even remaining silent or neutral for whatever reason, and one is quite correctly condemned. Even the Americans who helped to liberate the camps are criticized for not actively committing themselves to a policy of rescuing Jews, and the Jewish community itself in America and in Palestine is not spared investigation on this count. And yet, for reasons of state, the Israeli government, aided and abetted by many American Jews, pursues policies which seem to the oppressed to be quite similar. Bishop Tutu immediately sees a similarity between the Jewish Holocaust and apartheid, and yet it is no longer obvious to many in the Jewish community, at least in practical political and military actions.[36]

In religious terms, the inability to see the connection between our own suffering and the suffering of others may be related to a contemporary form of idolatry, an ancient Jewish insight that, like the Exodus and the prophets, has atrophied in the contemporary Jewish community and has been reclaimed by Christian liberation struggles.

Idolatry has at least two aspects: the problem of cultic images of

God and the worship of other, false gods. Pablo Richard, a Chilean biblist and sociologist, understands the first aspect of idolatry as a radical call to liberation found in the Exodus story. Affirmation of the transcendence of God is, at the same time, an affirmation of God's plan to liberate the people. A refusal to work for liberation is an act of idolatry—not the idolatry of false gods, but the idolatry that is possible only from within the worship of the true God. "In Exodus 32, God reveals his transcendence as God the liberator, and not a God who consoles the oppressed so that they will accept their condition as an oppressed people. The veneration of God as consoler is idolatry. The seat or throne of this god—where he reigns or manifests his presence to the people—is gold, and gold is the symbol of domination." At the same time, the oppressor is seen as an idolator as well: both the oppressed and the oppressor "practice an idolatry that deforms and perverts the revelation of the liberating transcendence of God."[37]

The prophets embody the critique of the second aspect of idolatry, refusing to worship false gods. The false gods are domination and excessive materialism; they take on a transcendent quality which displaces the liberating God. According to Richard, Isaiah 46:1–7 illustrates this understanding, the central idea being that the idolatrous have to "carry" their idols, whereas believers are carried, lifted, and liberated by Yahweh.[38]

Christian Scriptures continue and further the understanding of idolatry, and Richard sees the transcendent presence of God in humans, in nature, and in history as the most radical critique of idolatry. This transcendent and liberating presence of God in history is antagonistic to all idolatrous practices and all fabrication of idols, because now God's liberating deeds in history have been revealed. On the other hand, idolatry is revealed through the destruction of human beings and of nature to the extent that human beings make idols that allow them to manipulate powers and values, to use them against other human beings.[39]

The most interesting aspect of Richard's and of other Christian liberation theologians' discussion of idolatry is that they find idolatry in the Bible to be intimately linked to situations of political oppression. The refusal to be idolatrous is the refusal to place systems of domination over the human quest for compassion and solidarity. Stated another way, Christian liberation theologians assert that the God we worship is not defined by the prayers we say or the words used to justify activities in the world, but that the activity itself defines our God and commitment. When we face a system of domination whose rationale assumes a transcendent quality, the only honest response is to refuse to "worship" or participate in that system. Thus the refusal to be idolatrous can be seen as the willingness to be a-theistic. The question of idolatry, then, often does not begin with affirming transcendence but with breaking away from a false transcendence which legitimates oppression. Idolatry distorts judgment; breaking with idolatry opens the possibility of clarity and justice.

There is no doubt that parts of the Jewish community have their own recently acquired idols: capitalism, patriotism, and national security. We are increasingly taught to "believe" in America and Israel rather than critically embrace diverse Jewish communities. A high-ranking officer of a major Jewish denomination remarked once that Israel is a God in the Jewish community—and so it has become. That is why a rational discussion of Israel is so difficult today. Irving Greenberg's sense of Israel as a religious category thus describes the situation and yet portends doom. Could atheism toward Israel be a path of fidelity in which our own community is brought to account? In this crucial time, could the refusal to make of Israel an idol be a gesture of humility and hope rather than an unforgivable sin for which excommunication is the only answer?

Instead of being divisive, the refusal to engage in idolatry might actually begin healing our community; it might serve as a bridge between religious and secular Jews among whom the question shifts from belief in God to the values of a good and just life that we can mutually affirm. At the same time, the refusal of idolatry might become a bridge to other suffering communities where we together begin to emphasize the most powerful statement of Irving Greenberg, that after the Holocaust "no statement, theological or otherwise can be credible if it is not credible in the presence of burning children." "Burning children" at once becomes the central critique of unjust power and the path to a new form of solidarity. According to Greenberg, the victims ask the world above anything else "not to allow the creation of another matrix of values that might sustain another attempt at genocide." Is this not the place of meeting that demands an opening to other struggles, an opening that at the same time calls us to the depths of our own history?[40]

CHAPTER 5

Toward a Reconstruction of Jewish Life

Years after the liberation of the camps, Elie Wiesel wrote, "Were hatred a solution, the survivors, when they came out of the camps, would have had to burn down the whole world." In fact the world had already been burned down, and the survivors inherited a world emptied of values and much goodness, though the victors had difficulty recognizing the new landscape. Hannah Arendt, in her book *The Origins of Totalitarianism*, saw this clearly when she wrote of the end of Western civilization and the traditions that gave rise to and guided it. For Arendt, the Judeo-Christian traditions, as well as the humanist tradition, collapsed in the death camps of Nazi Germany: they not only failed to prevent this catastrophe; they in many ways contributed to the impetus for mass death. Because of this a new foundation for civilization was needed, and Arendt called for a consciously created philosophical and political structure that would renew—or at least make possible again—a civilization worthy of the name.[1]

Yet almost a half a century later, the difficulty of such an enterprise is ever present. In fact, many see the possibility of a new foundation in the renewal and transformation of the traditions that failed and are in disarray. Christian liberation movements are desperately and courageously addressing this question, and though they are a distinct minority among Christians, can one doubt that they are the hope of the future? A new Christian witness not only confronts its own propensity for domination; it lends strength, courage, and insight to other struggling communities, as we have seen. Still, it is critical to understand that Christian renewal did not come simply from within, but rather arose in dialogue with suffering communities, including the Jewish community, who posed unequivocally the critique of domination that could no longer be denied. Christian movements today are authentic only insofar as they carry the memory of their victims with them.

As we have seen, the Jewish tradition is hardly free from the onslaught of contemporary history; it struggles within the dialectics of Holocaust and empowerment, survival and ethics, exile and renewal. A strength, deservedly seen as remarkable, has emerged from the Holocaust world. At the same time we find a profound unease, often covered over with militant rhetoric and accusation. Proud of our achievements in economics and science, celebrating our new-found military prowess, we nevertheless feel the ground giving way beneath our feet. Togetherness is stressed as an ideal unto itself, while grafted to it is a profound sense of loneliness. Those Jews who struggle for renewal often do so without religious language or in a language that has hardly confronted the night. The religious language of empowerment is important, but it lacks the ability to critique; the religious language of renewal is neo-orthodox or fragmented, spoken to a small audience or in pre-Holocaust symbols that, in view of our contemporary history, are less and less adequate.

The voices of ethical concern such as Shorris and Feuerlicht are warnings to be taken seriously. Political dissent (such as civil disobedience) and feminist critique put ethical teaching in contact with everyday reality. Other movements, such as those of Christian liberation, are of help if we are humble enough to listen; recognition of the commonality of night, of the innocent suffering, is crucial. Ultimately, however, these are clues to a reconstruction that is only on the horizon: feared by some, expected by others, and yet unnamed.

Our history bequeaths the dialectic of Holocaust and empowerment as well as the tension and arguments found within it. But what are the borders of this dialectic for which the forces of renewal reach? Is there a way to move within and beyond the now-articulated tripartite reality of Holocaust, empowerment, and re-newal that elicits articulate rhetoric while allowing the present neoconservative direction to continue and perhaps even to acceler-ate? In a sense we have already suggested a way to challenge the Jewish community to move forward by solidarity with those who suffer. The desire to be in solidarity does not eliminate the dynam-ics of the Jewish community, but places them in a different perspec-tive. It has the possibility of moving us beyond isolation and liberal concern into an active community that finds its way by means of concrete acts of justice. Thus a new reference point emerges, and solidarity becomes the watchword.

Solidarity is the movement of the heart, mind, and body toward those who are suffering. Though often seen as a movement out-ward toward others, as something added on to a fulfilled life, solidarity actually is a journey to ourselves as well. It is an attempt to reclaim our own humanity, bruised and alienated when our lives are built on the exploitation of others. This is true of a solidarity with our own community as well, for the journey toward others is at the same time a journey toward the foundations of one's own community. One can posit the opposite: a person or community that refuses solidarity ultimately refuses itself. The Constantinian synthesis of church and state speaks clearly in this area: when Christianity became the empire's religion, it lost its soul. The Nazis became mirror images of the victims they created: lonely, anony-mous, dehumanized. In a very different way we see this possibility in the Jewish community today as empowerment overshadows the prophetic until it is banished, and with it a founding block of the Jewish spirit.[2]

Solidarity also means the willingness to enter into history with authenticity and fidelity. Entry into history is the willingness to engage in a critical dialogue with economic, social, political, and religious issues. Put simply, the critical dialogue is ongoing: some-times decisive, other times indeterminate. Rarely is there one an-swer; rather, there is a series of questions and decisions to be thought through and acted upon. A lived witness means to make a choice within the critical dialogue, to plant one's feet without all the answers, to choose a way of life in the mix of history. The critical dialogue informs lived witness with an open invitation to continue the search; the lived witness deepens the dialogue with a reality which calls forth commitment. Critical dialogue and lived witness are both individual and communal. The community can encourage or discourage individuals to enter into history, and the community itself can undergo the process of critical dialogue and lived witness, though this is rare.[3]

Whether a person or community views the present as a hostile environment to be transcended and defeated, or as a locus for solidarity, dialogue, and lived witness depends in large measure on how the past is viewed. The past is alive in the present through memory and myth; past events influence the life of a people as these events take on a formative character. The Holocaust and the founding of the State of Israel are two such formative events for the Jewish people.

While it is true that these two events, because of their power, broke through tradition as it had been given, they are now part and parcel of a new tradition. Tradition always has a tendency to become, in the words of Walter Benjamin, a Jewish philosopher, "a tool of the ruling classes"; that is, it begins to lose its power as a motivator toward solidarity. The events themselves critique injustice, displacement, and murder even though time and human agencies dull the critical edge: they may approve what they once critiqued. Hence Benjamin's comment: "In every era the attempt must be made anew to wrest tradition away from a conformism that is about to overpower it."[4]

For Benjamin this is the task of the historian, who, recognizing that the "image of enslaved ancestors" allows both hatred and a spirit of sacrifice, seeks to recover the past as an impetus for solidarity in the present. Benjamin writes: "The past carries with it a temporal index by which it is referred to redemption. There is a secret agreement between past generations and the present one. Our coming was expected on earth. Like every generation that preceded us, we have been endowed with a *weak* Messianic power, a power to which the past has a claim. That claim cannot be settled cheaply." Benjamin concludes, "Only that historian will have the gift of fanning the spark of hope in the past who is firmly convinced that *even the dead* will not be safe from the enemy if he wins. And this enemy has not ceased to be victorious."[5]

Thus to Benjamin the past, as recalled in the present, has two possibilities: to legitimate or to critique unjust power. The tendency is to conformism, but this robs the past of its authenticity and in so doing robs the dead of their voice. Certain actions, although performed in behalf of persecuted persons, actually serve to affirm the persecutors. The task of the historian is to allow the voices of the suffering to be heard, particularly by their children, who, while venerating their oppressed ancestors, tend to ignore their cries by persecuting others. The memory of enslaved ancestors thus subverts traditions of conformism to power. Empowerment is possible, but those who are empowered must bear in mind that solidarity with those suffering in the present is the only link with suffering in the past, and to ignore or cause suffering is to lose the raison d'être of empowerment. Even more dangerous is the emerging solidarity that follows: solidarity with other victors. Benjamin writes that "all rulers are the heirs of those who conquered before them" and "whoever has emerged victorious participates to this day in the triumphal procession in which the present rulers step over those who are lying prostrate." That is why the historian regards it as his or her task to "brush history against the grain."[6]

For Benjamin, the recovery of suffering is subversive and is carried out by those willing to brush against the grain of acceptable speech and activity. Conformism is the way of betrayal; fidelity is the critique of the victorious by way of committed thought and activity that takes seriously the dead and those dying in the present. Not surprisingly, it is this difficult struggle to be faithful that, for Benjamin, is the stirring of theology, "the straight gate through which the Messiah might enter."[7]

To recover the memory of suffering is to probe again what is now assumed, to analyze what has been elevated to the sacred. We are alerted to a diversity where we now see only monolith; we uncover paths untravelled though once suggested. The present loses its univocal quality as the choices of the past are brought into view. The understanding of fidelity is broadened considerably, and the possibility of reconciliation emerges. Reconciliation is understood here not only in terms of the enemy, but in terms of oneself and community. Past and current events take on a new shading where forgiveness as well as humility is possible. Such memories challenge the victim and the victor alike even when they seem to have changed places. Reconciliation portends transformation.[8]

Two figures who challenge present Jewish sensibility are Etty

Hillesum and Martin Buber. As persons living within the formative events of contemporary Jewish life, the Holocaust and the founding of the State of Israel, they viewed their situations quite differently from the way Jewish consensus allows today. Hillesum elicits a spirituality that is difficult for us to understand. She evokes a familiarity with God that major theologians of our community find almost impossible. Hillesum seems almost to accept the fate of her people as inevitable or, perhaps more accurately, rises to heroic stature within the parameters of the moment. Though in and around the borders of her life we hear the familiar refrain "Never Again," we also hear other voices, including the poetic and the language of God. She is shocking in her simplicity, in her acceptance, and in her prayer. Buber, on the other hand, as an exile from Germany and a settler in Palestine, is a voice of empowerment, though in tones less familiar to us today. Buber was a great Biblicist, philosopher and educator, but what concerns us here is his unequivocal stand for rapprochement with his Arab neighbors. Buber's theology underlay these positions and was equally scandalous: one of the most famous religious Jews in the world rarely attended synagogue, and he understood that deed and encounter called for confederation with, rather than domination of, the Arab population.

ETTY HILLESUM

Etty Hillesum was born on January 15, 1914, in Middleburg, Holland, where her father, Dr. L. Hillesum, taught classical languages. Dr. Hillesum was an excellent and disciplined scholar who prized an orderly life, while Etty's mother, Rebecca Bernstein, was passionate and driven; having fled Russian pogroms, she migrated to The Netherlands. Though the marriage was quite tempestuous, Etty and her brothers, Mischa and Jaap, were intelligent and gifted. Mischa was a brilliant musician considered to be one of the most promising pianists in Europe, while Jaap discovered some new vitamins when he was a teenager and later became a doctor. Etty took her first degree in law at the University of Amsterdam and then enrolled in the Faculty of Slavonic Languages. When the Second World War broke out, she had already turned to the study of psychology.

At the time she started writing her diaries, Holland was increasingly under the domination of Nazi Germany, and with Holland's surrender in the spring of 1940, Germany began to isolate the Dutch Jews. Despite resistance to those measures by the Dutch, Jews were gathered into ghettos and work camps. In the spring of 1942, Jews were forced to wear the Star of David, and wholesale deportations began. Westerbork, a transit camp in the east of the Netherlands, was designated as the last stop before the extermination camp, Auschwitz.

By July 1942, Hillesum found work as a typist in a department of the Jewish Council, a body formed at Nazi instigation to handle Jewish affairs. In essence, the Nazis gave orders to the Council and then let it decide how to implement them. Fourteen days after she started work, Hillesum volunteered to go with the first group of Jews to Westerbork. As the editor of her diaries, J. G. Gaarlandt writes, "She did not want to escape the fate of the Jewish people. She believed that she could do justice to life only if she did not abandon those in danger, and if she used her strength to bring light into the life of others."[9]

From August 1942 until September 1943 Hillesum remained in Westerbork camp with a new job in the local hospital. Because of a special permit from the Jewish Council she was able on occasion to travel to Amsterdam, where she brought letters and messages to people and was able to procure medicines for the camp. Though her health was poor and friends encouraged her to escape, she refused. On September 7, 1943, Hillesum—along with her parents and brother, Mischa—was transported to Auschwitz, where she died on November 30. Her parents and Mischa died there too; her other brother Jaap survived the camp but died returning to Holland.[10]

Hillesum's diaries are filled with passion and an almost mystical simplicity. Her spirituality is eclectic and beautiful, though in some ways disturbing. Rilke and Dostoevsky are her spiritual guides, as are the Jewish and Christian Scriptures. In a harrowing time Hillesum is open to the world, unafraid of exploring its treasures. Suffering and beauty, existing side-by-side, encourage reflections on life and destiny. Throughout, her guide is compassion, though increasingly a compassion tried through fire.

The testimony of such a life is startling. On June 25, 1942, Hillesum reflects on Nazi brutality.

They are merciless, totally without pity. And we must be all the more merciful ourselves. That's why I prayed early this morning: "Oh God, times are too hard for frail people like myself. I know that a new and kinder day will come. I would so much like to live on, if only to express all the love I carry with me. And there is only one way of preparing the new age, by living it even now in our hearts. Somewhere in me I feel so light, without the least bitterness and so full of strength and love. I would so much like to help prepare the new age."

That's how it went, more or less, my prayer this morning. I suddenly had to kneel down on the hard coconut matting in the bathroom and the tears poured down my face. And that prayer gave me enough strength for the rest of the day.[11]

It is within the context of her time that Hillesum's prayers continue and deepen. In Westerbork on August 18, 1943, just three weeks before her death, she wrote:

My life has become an uninterrupted dialogue with You, oh God, one great dialogue. Sometimes when I stand in some corner of the camp, my feet planted on Your earth, my eyes raised towards Your Heaven, tears sometimes run down my face, tears of deep emotion and gratitude. At night, too, when I lie in my bed and rest in You, oh God, tears of gratitude run down my face, and that is my prayer. I have been terribly tired for several days, but that, too, will pass; things come and go in a deeper rhythm and people must be taught to listen to it, it is the most important thing we have to learn in this life. I am not challenging You, oh God, my life is one great dialogue with You. I may never become the great artist I would really like to be, but I am already secure in You, God. Sometimes I try my hand at turning out small profundities and uncertain short stories, but I always end up with just one single word: God. And that says everything and there is no need for anything more.[12]

Hillesum's prayers to God are filled with questions. God may be powerless to help the Jewish people, but can Jews help God? Here a mystical element becomes central. Her diary entry of July 12, 1942, begins with this meditation:

> Dear God, these are anxious times. Tonight for the first time I lay in the dark with burning eyes as scene after scene of human suffering passed before me. I shall promise You one thing, God, just one very small thing: I shall never burden my today with cares about my tomorrow, although that takes some practice. Each day is sufficient unto itself. I shall try to help You, God, to stop my strength ebbing away, though I cannot vouch for it in advance. But one thing is becoming increasingly clear to me: that You cannot help us, that we must help You to help ourselves. And that is all we can manage these days and also all that really matters: that we safeguard that little piece of You, God, in ourselves. And perhaps in others as well. Alas, there doesn't seem to be much You Yourself can do about our circumstances, about our lives. Neither do I hold You responsible. You cannot help us but we must help You and defend Your dwelling place inside us to the last.[13]

If Hillesum had isolated herself from her people, these prayers, even her dialogue with God, would sound empty, almost arrogant. Their power comes from the commitment for which she gave her life. For Hillesum it was quite simply being faithful.

> I shall always be able to stand on my own two feet even when they are planted on the hardest soil of the harshest reality. And my acceptance is not indifference or helplessness. I feel deep moral indignation at a regime that treats human beings in such a way. But events have become too overwhelming and too demonic to be stemmed with personal resentment and bitterness. These responses strike me as being utterly childish and unequal to the fateful course of events. People often get worked up when I say it doesn't really matter whether I go or somebody else does, the main thing is that so many thousands have to go. It is not as if I want to fall into the arms of destruction with a resigned smile—far from it, I am only

bowing to the inevitable and even as I do so I am sustained by the certain knowledge that ultimately they cannot rob us of anything that matters. But I don't think I would feel happy if I were exempted from what so many others have to suffer. They keep telling me that someone like me has a duty to go into hiding, because I have so many things to do in life, so much to give. But I know that whatever I may have to give to others, I can give it no matter where I am, here in the circle of my friends or over there, in a concentration camp. And it is sheer arrogance to think oneself too good to share the fate of the masses.[14]

For many Jews these prayers are impossible to utter after Auschwitz, yet they were offered on the rails to Auschwitz and no doubt in the camp as well. To be sure, her understandings are disturbing: is her God the God of the Exodus, or the God of Rilke? Passages from the Christian Scriptures are evoked, and though she herself does not indicate a preference, Christians reading into her diaries might find a latent follower of Jesus. Her journey, however, yields much more than these retrospective problems.

There is no hint from Hillesum that the suffering of her people is justified or divinely ordained, but there is a sense that fidelity within suffering opens the possibility of a new age. Barbarism is overwhelming; to hold on to the human, to acknowledge beauty, to continue to pray is to begin the transformation of travail into goodness. For Hillesum, Jews are not going like lambs to the slaughter, as is often said today. Instead we find unfolding a witness to the degradation and possibility of the human. The fate of the Jewish people, already decided by forces beyond their control, has an inner meaning that only the experience of suffering can impart. Martyrdom occurs without bitterness and with a commitment beyond ordinary comprehension. To accompany her people, to continue to pray, to listen to the stories of her compatriots is to resist the ultimate triumph of Nazism with every fiber of her being. For Hillesum, resistance unto death *is* the preparation for a future beyond Nazism.[15]

It is in the midst of suffering and commitment that Hillesum understands the beauty of creation and the goodness of life. The Kingdom of Death remains, though permeated with the sacredness of creation. Is this a contradiction that cannot now be spoken, or a paradox that bespeaks a healing that open levels of understanding beneath a justifiable internal and external hardening?

Survival as a people is nowhere mentioned in the diaries; perhaps this is presumed. Empowerment seems farther from her mind. Is it that she does not realize the extremity of the situation of Jews worldwide, or can she even imagine an empowered Jewish presence in Palestine? Whatever the answer, Hillesum's central theme is witness, not empowerment. Can we speak of this emphasis today without hesitation and shame, as if her view was naive and even dangerous? Finally, and most difficult, is Hillesum's emerging sense of forgiveness that undergirds her refusal to hate even the enemy. Her solidarity with the Jewish people extends to those caught up in a system that dehumanizes and in effect murders the conquerors as well. Hillesum's March 21, 1941 extended diary entry is, in the face of her impending death, as remarkable as it is controversial.

What a bizarre new landscape, so full of eerie fascination, yet one we might also come to love again. We human beings cause monstrous conditions, but precisely because we cause them we soon learn to adapt ourselves to them. Only if we become such that we can no longer adapt ourselves, only if, deep inside, we rebel against every kind of evil, will we be able to put a stop to it. Aeroplanes, streaking down in flames, still have a weird fascination for us—even aesthetically—though we know, deep down, that human beings are being burnt alive. As long as that happens, while everything within us does not yet scream out in protest, so long will we find ways of adapting ourselves, and the horror will continue. Does that mean I am never sad, that I never rebel, always acquiesce, and love life no matter what the circumstances? No, far from it. I believe that I know and share the many sorrows and sad circumstances that a human being can experience, but I do not cling to them, I do not prolong such moments of agony. They pass through me, like life itself, as a broad, eternal stream, they become part of that stream, and life continues. And as a result all my strength is preserved, does not become tagged on to futile sorrow or rebelliousness.

And finally: ought we not, from time to time, open ourselves up to cosmic sadness? One day I shall surely be able to say to Ilse Blumenthal, "Yes, life is beautiful, and I value it anew at the end of every day, even though I know that the sons of mothers, and you are one such mother, are being murdered in concentration camps. And you must be able to bear your sorrow: even if it seems to crush you, you will be able to stand up again, for human beings are so strong, and your sorrow must become an integral part of yourself, part of your body and your soul, you mustn't run away from it, but bear it like an adult. Do not relieve your feelings through hatred, do not seek to be avenged on all German mothers, for they, too, sorrow at this very moment for their slain and murdered sons. Give your sorrow all the space and shelter in yourself that is its due, for if everyone bears his grief honestly and courageously, the sorrow that now fills the world will abate. But if you do not clear a decent shelter for your sorrow, and instead reserve most of the space inside you for hatred and thoughts of revenge—from which new sorrows will be born for others—then sorrow will never cease in this world and will multiply. And if you have given sorrow the space its gentle origins demand, then you may truly say: life is beautiful and so rich. So beautiful and so rich that it makes you want to believe in God."[16]

Hillesum's journey is recalled here, not because it was or should be paradigmatic for the Jewish people, but because it brushes against the grain of acceptable testimony. As Wiesel asserts, the Jewish survivors did not find hatred a solution. However, it is also true that the path to God and the possibility of forgiveness have been difficult, if not impossible. How do we trust a God who could not or did not deliver us from the death camps? How can we possibly forgive those who constructed the camps with their own hands, often with an incomprehensible joy? Certainly there are no answers here, only the willingness to allow disparate voices to be heard in their authenticity. Hillesum's is a lonely voice, though to be sure not the only voice, which exists on the borders of our understanding of the Holocaust.

MARTIN BUBER

Martin Buber was another such voice on the periphery of Jewish consciousness and activity, though from a certain vantage point it may be hard to discern him as anything if not central to the Jewish community. Born in 1878 to a wealthy Austrian family, by the 1930s Buber was well known throughout Europe as a Jewish theologian and scholar. As the Nazi period began, Buber became an outspoken opponent of Hitler and finally left for Palestine in 1938. His journey there was in the first instance forced by Nazism, though Zionism was hardly new to him. From the early part of the century he perceived the need for the revival of Jewish culture in the ancient home of the Jewish people. His Zionism, however, had a striking caveat: the success of the Jewish return to Palestine would be measured by relations with the Arab population. For Buber, Palestine was to be shared by those who returned and those indigenous to that land.[17]

The case for the Jewish return to the land is made over and over again in Buber's works. One example is his testimony in March 1946 before an Anglo-American Inquiry Committee formed to explore the British Mandate, specifically the plight of Jewish survivors of the Nazi Holocaust and the possibility of their immigration to Palestine. Buber begins by relating modern political Zionism to the ancient birth of the Jewish people. For Buber, modern political Zionism was prompted and intensified, but not caused, by modern anti-Semitism. Zionism attested to the unique connection of a people and a country. The Jewish people were created by the power of a tradition founded on the promise made to them during their wanderings in the desert: the promise of Canaan as their "heritage." According to Buber this tradition was decisive for the history of humankind in that it "confronted the new people with a task they could carry out only as a people, namely to establish in Canaan a model and 'just' community." Later the prophets interpreted this task as obliging the community to carry social and political justice throughout the world. Thereby the most productive and most paradoxical of all human ideas, messianism, was offered to humanity.

It placed the people of Israel in the center of an activity leading towards the advent of the Kingdom of God on earth, an activity in which all the peoples were to cooperate. It ordered every generation to contribute to the upbuilding of the sacred future with the forces and resources at their command. . . . Within the people that had created it, this idea grew to a force of quite peculiar vitality. Driven out of their promised land, this people survived nearly two millennia by their trust in their return, in the fulfillment of the promise, in the realization of the idea. The inner connection with this land and the belief in the promised reunion with it were a permanent force of rejuvenation for this people, living in conditions which probably would have caused the complete disintegration of any other group.[18]

From this analysis flow what Buber considers the three irreducible demands of Zionism. First, the freedom to acquire land in sufficient quantity to bring about a renewed connection with the "primal form of production," from which the Jewish people had been separated for centuries and without which "no original spiritual and social productivity can arise." Second, a powerful influx of settlers, especially of youth, to strengthen and revive the work of reconstruction and to protect it from the dangers of stagnancy and isolation. Third, self-determination of the Jewish community about its way of life and the form of its institutions, as well as an assurance for its unimpeded development as a community.[19]

For Buber these demands also produced obligations: justice for and within a community must be carried out without threatening the rights of any other community. Independence of one could hardly be gained at the expense of another. "Jewish settlement must oust no Arab peasant, Jewish immigration must not cause the political status of the present inhabitants to deteriorate, and must continue to ameliorate their economic condition." Buber saw the aim of a regenerated Jewish people in Palestine as twofold: to live peacefully with the inhabitants of the land and to cooperate with Palestinians in opening and developing the land. As Buber wrote, "Such cooperation is an indispensable condition for the lasting success of the great work, of the redemption of this land."[20]

Buber saw the cooperative basis as offering room for both the

Jewish and the Palestinian people, and though this necessitated autonomy, the demand for a Jewish state or a Jewish majority was of less importance.

> We need for this land as many Jews as it is possible economically to absorb, but not in order to establish a majority against a minority. We need them because great, very great forces are required to do the unprecedented work. We need for this land a solid, vigorous, autonomous community, but not in order that it should give its name to a state; we need it because we want to raise Israel and *Eretz Israel* to the highest level of productivity they can be raised to. The new situation and the problem involved ask for new solutions that are beyond the capacity of the familiar political categories. An internationally guaranteed agreement between the two communities is asked for, which defines the spheres of interest and activity common to the partners and those not common to them, and guarantees mutual non-interference for these specific spheres.[21]

Early on, Buber saw two opposing tendencies within Zionism that correspond to two different interpretations of the concept of national rebirth. The first was to understand national rebirth as the intention to restore the true Israel where spirit and life would no longer be separated as in the Diaspora. Rather, spirit and life would come together in Israel's ancient homeland. The second saw rebirth as normalization: the need for land, language, and independence such as any nation needed. For Buber this latter interpretation displayed an interest in acquiring the commodities of nationhood but failed to consider the important questions: How will people live with one another in this land? What will people say to one another in the renewed Hebrew language? What will be the connection of their independence with the rest of humanity? Two conflicting tendencies were inherited from ancient times: "the powerful consciousness of the task of maintaining truth and justice in the total life of the nation, internally and externally, and thus becoming an example and a light to humanity; and the natural desire, all too natural, to be "like the nations." According to Buber, the ancient Hebrews never succeeded in becoming a normal nation. Two weeks after the Proclamation of Independence in May, 1948, Buber reported, "Today Jews are succeeding at it to a terrifying degree."[22]

Buber continued to protest Israeli nationalism until his death in 1965. While it is true that he was never alone in his hopes and disappointments, Buber can honestly be seen as an exile in a land he participated in building. His confederationist and bi-national proposals fell on deaf ears. By the end of Buber's life his vision of religious socialism was hardly understood or considered. Though dissenting minorities within Israel continue to criticize their government's policies, the road taken by the State of Israel is quite different from the one proposed by Buber. His understandings are regarded as utopian, untenable, and even dangerous for a modern state. The security of Israel is defined as distinct over and against that of the Palestinian people, and since the Six-Day War new territories have been acquired. Normalization continues unabated as the arms industry becomes the leading earner of foreign currency; the foreign-policy involvements in the Middle East and elsewhere would have horrified Buber in their magnitude and cynicism.[23]

Buber's understandings challenge the contemporary Jewish community in many ways. For Buber, the return to Palestine is a spiritual act, a religious category, as it were, the essence of which is regeneration rather than survival. Regeneration occurs in relation to history, to the land, and to the people who inherited the land; autonomy signals authenticity and the ability to enter into relationship rather than the ability to go it alone. Regeneration represents the rebirth of Jewish witness and values: survival without witness can only be seen as failure.

To be sure, Buber's thought raises many questions. Buber assumed the right of Jews to become an autonomous force in Palestine; but was this possible in the historical situation without a state and its concomitant militarization? Friendship and cooperation are built on mutual give and take; but did either the Jews or the Palestinians at that moment of history have the inner resources to come into relation? Most of the Zionists were secular Jews and saw religion as a bulwark against change. Could Buber's religious socialism have appealed to a people longing to reclaim itself within the realm of economics and politics? The inhabitants of Palestine also raised questions: Was not Buber's sense of Jewish mission really the continuation of European colonialism, albeit in a more friendly manner? Though less than most settlers, Buber retained a sense of paternalism toward his Arab neighbors, and his sense of development, though socialist and decentralized, was still based on a European rather than a Middle Eastern model.

THE DIFFICULT PATH OF HILLESUM AND BUBER

As with Hillesum, the questions remain and the answers are less important. The memory of Martin Buber brushes recent Jewish history against the grain. He represents a choice as yet untaken, a path almost disappeared from view. Can his understandings be broached in the Jewish community today, or is his life a dangerous memory better left alone? Still, he represents the possibility of reconciliation with the Palestinians as well as with our own history. Buber calls for a fundamental turning away from domination to relation, which is at the same time peace with the Palestinian people and a recovery of the Jewish witness in Israel and Palestine. Buber's voice, however, extends far beyond the Middle East. Would not his views, like Hillesum's, call for a reevaluation of Jewish understandings in North America as well?

Buber's understanding of empowerment as intimately linked with solidarity is bound to the reality of God, and here Buber is at his most challenging. For Buber, tradition names God too easily, objectifying what is mysterious and nameless. In his pre-Holocaust writings, Buber seeks to establish for the Jewish people an existential relation with God through exploration of subjectivity and nature. God is revealed to the person through history, individually and in community. God calls for *teshuvah*, repentance and turning toward self, neighbor, and nature. The human responds with decision and deed that illustrate *teshuvah*. A path is before us; it is up to us to choose it. Even as we move in another direction the path remains to be chosen again. The path is a form of solidarity with creation and history; the locus of fidelity becomes a "mysterious approach to closeness."[24]

The post-Holocaust theology Buber posits is less certain than his previous theology, though the basic outlines remain the same. The difficulty of belief is understandable, and to force belief is dishonest. Still, the path of trust and solidarity remains, and righteous activity may once again bring the center of Jewish life into focus. For who has banished God if not humans themselves?

> Such is the nature of this hour. But what of the next? It is a modern superstition that the character of an age acts as fate for the next. One lets it prescribe what is possible to do and hence what is permitted. One surely cannot swim against the stream, one says. But perhaps one can swim with a new stream whose source is still hidden? In another image, the I-Thou relation has gone into the catacombs—who can say with how much greater power it will step forth! Who can say when the I-It relation will be directed anew to its assisting place and activity!
>
> The most important events in the history of that embodied possibility called man are the occasionally occurring beginnings of new epochs, determined by forces previously invisible or unregarded. Each age is, of course, a continuation of the preceding one, but a continuation can be confirmation and it can be refutation.
>
> Something is taking place in the depths that as yet needs no name. To-morrow even it may happen that it will be beckoned to from the heights, across the heads of the earthly archons. The eclipse of the light of God is no extinction; even to-morrow that which has stepped in between may give way.[25]

Could it be that the reestablishment of trust will allow the difficult post-Holocaust questions to be raised again in a spirit of search and fellowship? The eclipse of God felt by women and men of our age is a reality which, if unaddressed, allows the carnage to continue. Could solidarity be a response to this eclipse that one day may allow the question of God to be raised in a different, more relevant way?

There is no doubt that the path of solidarity that Hillesum and Buber suggest is a difficult one, especially when the lessons of Jewish history counsel against it. After the Holocaust and the struggle to establish an autonomous presence in Palestine, trust is often seen as naive and dangerous. Still, Hillesum and Buber caution us that hatred and isolation lead to bitterness without solace and ultimately to survival without witness. The fact that within the Holocaust and the founding of the State of Israel there were Jews who prayed and struggled, dissented and trusted reminds us that generosity often occurs in the most unexpected places—when we are least secure—and that, paradoxically, the hardening occurs when the community achieves power. Surely the demands are different within empowerment, but the raison d'être of empowerment found in the struggle and generosity of enslaved ancestors is in danger of being lost. The lives of Hillesum and Buber echo the challenge of Walter Benjamin to rescue tradition from conformity to power, a power that becomes the tool of the ruling class. They suggest that to move from one oppression to another, in spite of the rationale, is to forget our history and, ultimately, to denigrate ourselves as a people.

Today we desperately need a new angle of vision, and thus the reconstruction of Jewish life begins with the forgotten and the peripheral, with the unasked questions and the assumed answers. Hillesum and Buber provide this different angle of vision because they carry within them parts of our heritage that languish in the present. They embody a language of the heart formed in the midst of Jewish history, a language almost frightening to speak of today. If it is true, however, that the way back is covered with the blood of our ancestors, a future without the possibility of God and of reconciliation is bleak indeed. Could Hillesum and Buber and the many others like them provide, in Benjamin's words, the "weak messianic spark" of which we are in such great need and through which a renewed Jewish life might emerge?

CHAPTER 6

From Holocaust to Solidarity: Toward a Jewish Theology of Liberation

Jewish theology arises out of and is accountable to the experience of the people. Its function is threefold: to articulate significant moments in Jewish history; to become a guide for direction and choice in the present; and to provide the resources necessary to create a future for the Jewish people. The present incorporates the past as a guide and witness. Memory serves as an anchor to those who have gone before us and as a critical reminder of the difficult path of fidelity. The future emerges from the binding together of memory and contemporary choice, sometimes in a slavish way, other times in the way of freedom. While mooring us, the past can also set us free. Once we are sure of where we have come from, sure of who we are, this rootedness allows us to explore, to rethink, to move forward even in dangerous times.

Theology that has arisen from the Holocaust experience is of overwhelming importance. Like Elie Wiesel, Richard Rubenstein, and Emil Fackenheim, Irving Greenberg quite rightly places the Holocaust alongside the Exodus event and the rabbinic interpretations in its scope and honesty. Many, perhaps a majority of Jews

110

preferred that the painful Holocaust would remain unnamed and the abyss fade from view. Similarly, the State of Israel was in the beginning opposed by some of the Orthodox and Reform Jews and by more than a few of the Conservative movement. Until the 1967 Six-Day War, North American Jews approached Israel in the light of charity and of the bonds Jews feel with other Jews, but with nowhere near the uncritical consensus one sees today. Yet Jewish theologians presented the story of Israel as intrinsic to the renewal of Jewish life. As theologians they refused the pious sphere of prayer and good deeds and spoke publicly about the need for empowerment as a religious response to destruction.[1]

However, along the way the articulation of Jewish concerns and aspiration lost its edge. Perhaps the consensus that Holocaust theology responded to and helped to form blunted the theology's critical edge. Perhaps Holocaust theology is awaiting a new theology to continue the work it so nobly began. The Holocaust theologians were a daring generation, criticized and heralded; their legacy is a lasting one. They did not arise from the centers of Jewish power and influence, but from the periphery of organized Jewish life. They took the Jewish establishment by surprise and turned it upside down. Today a new generation of Jewish theologians is needed. Buoyed by the movements of ethical concern and renewal previously cited and informed by the witness of Hillesum and Buber, they, like the Holocaust theologians, must emerge from the periphery of Jewish life to challenge a consensus that admits of little dissent.[2]

THE CHALLENGES OF A NEW THEOLOGY

Though it is impossible to state definitively what kind of theology will emerge, major themes that have surfaced in our discussion of contemporary Jewish life are worthy of note. They help to define the parameters of Jewish theology and thereby may well elicit further clarification of the future of the Jewish community as the twentieth century comes to a close.

First, a contemporary Jewish theology feels a tension between particularity and universality as a self-critical voice that comes from the depths of the Jewish tradition and seeks to serve the world. It must be distinctly Jewish in category and speech yet generous toward other religious and humanist communities.

Second, Jewish theology needs to acknowledge that genuine affirmation comes only through critical discourse and responsible activity in light of historical events. It must seek to be present in history rather than pretending to isolation or transcendence.

Third, Jewish theology has to emphasize inclusivity (e.g., religious and secular Jews, women and men), a search for a renewal of community life in the midst of Holocaust and empowerment, and the refusal to be silent despite pressure from political and religious neoconservatives for a moratorium on critique of the Jewish community.

Fourth, Jewish theology has no choice but to balance the survival of the Jewish people with the preservation of its message of community. It is compelled to assert that survival and preservation of its essential message are ultimately one and the same thing: there is no survival in any meaningful sense without a deepening of the witness its values offer to the world.

Fifth, Jewish theology requires the recovery of Jewish witness against idolatry as testimony to life in its private and public dimensions, as the essential bond of Jews everywhere, and as the fundamental link to religious and humanist communities of good will around the globe.

Finally, Jewish theology must in its essence be a call to *teshuvah:* commitment and solidarity in all their pain and possibility, as well as a critical understanding of the history we are creating and the courage it takes to change the course of that history.

Within an emerging Jewish theology of liberation, the revivial of the prophetic and the pursuit of liberation is critical. Though these carry qualities found in the very origins of the Jewish community, our discussion demonstrates that their recovery must occur within the welter of our time: the prophetic and liberation themes confront the dialectic of Holocaust and empowerment, deepening the themes of renewal and solidarity already present. Prophetic Jewish theology, or a Jewish theology of liberation, seeks to bring to light the hidden and sometimes censored movements of Jewish life. It seeks to express the dissent of those afraid or unable to speak. Ultimately, a Jewish theology of liberation seeks, in concert with others, to weave disparate hopes and aspirations into the very heart of Jewish life. Can a Jewish theology of liberation become the catalyst to break through the paralysis confronting the Jewish community today? Can it again ask the questions that are "resolved"? Can it challenge viewpoints inscribed in stone and the monuments now being erected and worshiped, often at the expense of our values and the life of others? And can this be done not to disparage or despair of the Jewish community, but in the deepest solidarity with it and with our history and our future?[3]

To be sure, though a Jewish theology of liberation begins on the periphery of Jewish life, it carries a past and present with it. The voices of the Exodus movement and of the prophets, of the martyrs who went to their death with a prayer to God and of those who refused prayer, of those who resisted with arms and those who resisted with the written word, are before us. The Holocaust theologians and the movements of renewal in North America and Israel are with us. And in the night, if we plumb the night's depths, the people of Guatemala, Nicaragua, and El Salvador, the people struggling in South Africa are with us too. Or so it could be, one day. Could it be that in our struggle we are not alone but are living rather in a broader tradition of faith and struggle, one that now seeks to galvanize the witness of each community and to share it with other struggling communities in a common struggle for liberation?[4]

And yet we are reminded again and again that, although our own movement toward solidarity is flawed, there are many, even among those who struggle for justice, who fear and dislike Jews. The generation of Nazis lives on; recent revelation of former United Nations Secretary General Kurt Waldheim's participation in the Nazi party and of his connection with atrocities is only one of many reminders for the Jewish people. Progressive Catholics welcome Jews as individuals but often ask that their Jewish particularity be left at the door. One need not travel far to run into the young Catholic priest who would die for a peasant in El Salvador but who admits to being anti-Semitic, or to hear a cocktail-hour discussion of dirty atheistic Jews. Although Louis Farakhan, the Black Muslim leader, rightly horrifies many with his anti-Semitic diatribes, it is the tone rather than the substance that is unique. What if a Jewish critique of Israel, for example, uttered with integrity and concern, is used to reinforce ancient prejudices against one's own people? Or if the critique of Jewish affluence is used to substantiate the continuing allegations of Jewish control of the world economy? What do you say, as a Jew who seeks solidarity with suffering persons, when Christian liberationists ask you to explain (in a friendly, informative manner, as if you have the "inside scoop" because of your heritage) how it came to be that "Jews control the media"? Surely the double standard continues unabated: Ariel Sharon symbolizes a fascist militarism and is identified as Jewish; but is Harry Truman, who ordered the atomic bombing on Hiroshima and Nagasaki, identified as a Christian or, for that matter, is Richard Nixon or Ronald Reagan? More often, "American President" is the prefix, and when "Christian" is affixed, a denial of their authentic Christianity occurs. And yet would not our analysis raise a similar question vis-à-vis Sharon's Jewishness? Would we be able to admit that such a perversion of our values—as represented by Ariel Sharon—arose in the Jewish community?[5]

A Jewish theology of liberation must insist that the issue of anti-Semitism survives and be confronted at every opportunity. At the same time, however, it must refuse to use anti-Semitism as an ideological weapon to instill fear and counter legitimate criticism. The slogan "Never Again" too often becomes the rationale for refusing to trust and to risk. It also blinds us to the fact that we have fostered an anti-Semitism of our own by our treatment of the Palestinian and Arab peoples, who are, after all, Semitic people. It might just be that the real anti-Semitism of the day is found neither in the United Nations nor in the Jewish critique of Israel, but in the Jewish community, where images of the unwashed, the ignorant and the terrorist are repeated *ad nauseam.* And if the Palestinian people's refusal to accept occupation on the West Bank and Gaza is somehow seen as anti-Semitic, could we also say that Israel's refusal to recognize and negotiate with the Palestine Liberation Organization is equally anti-Semitic?[6]

This is also true with reference to Blacks in the United States. Regardless of our history and how we interpret it, there is no question of who, in contemporary American life, is placed on the bottom of priority and opportunity. Although anti-Semitism assuredly exists in the Black community of North America, we cannot ignore the ugly fact that racism keeps Black North Americans on the margins of society. For too many Jews, a statement from a Black leader absolves us of our own social responsibilities and blinds us to the benefits we derive from a racist society. Anti-Semitism becomes a shield that deflects the difficult questions confronting us. A Jewish theology of liberation needs to turn the fact of anti-Semitism into a challenge for reflection and critical social analysis.

If anti-Semitism is seen as a challenge for the Jewish community, then the constructive efforts of Christians to overcome anti-Semitism become helpfully instructive. One thinks of many Christians in this regard, but feminist theologians are at the forefront. Both Rosemary Radford Ruether and Elisabeth Schüssler Fiorenza provide a provocative analyses of the rise of anti-Semitism. They probe the annals of patriarchy to answer whether or not anti-Semitism is a function of patriarchal consciousness and structure, and they caution the contemporary women's movement that the division of Christian and Jew represents a patriarchal intrusion into the lives of women, who need unity to fight a common enemy.[7]

Ultimately, a Jewish theology of liberation must engage the Christian community and admit the possibility of a Christian witness that, mindful of its anti-Jewish past and its complicity in many forms of domination, seeks to renew and even transform itself. First, however, we must speak to each other in the language of the heart and the mind. Is it possible that one day we could embrace both our differences and our commonality? This may be the most radical solidarity of all as well as the most healing, for the Jewish community gave birth to a Christian community that has not only forsaken its progenitor, but has also tried to destroy it. A great violence was done to our people in that tragic parting of ways, a violence extending to themes and persons within our tradition that today are still unspoken. At the same time, the Jewish foundation of the followers of Jesus was torn away and the erratic, often tragic history of Christianity suggests a need for Christians to reclaim their Hebraic heritage. Could the Holocaust become the catalyst for healing a brokenness that has plagued both communities for almost two thousand years? Recent books by Jewish authors point to such a possibility on the faith level, and a Jewish theology of liberation needs to explore such a journey in the realm of social and political life as well.[8]

The question of empowerment is hardly difficult in and of itself; the form and manner of empowerment is the crux of the discussion. A Jewish theology of liberation affirms empowerment with the proviso that one must affirm the empowerment of others as well. Israel, as an autonomous and powerful presence in the Middle East, is firmly established. What is needed, however, is the story of Israel's empowerment, a story that includes the injustices inflicted on the Palestinian people.

The counterpart to Israel as an autonomous presence is Palestine, and a Jewish theology of liberation begins to speak of Israel and Palestine together. That Israel is a state has less to do with religious principles than with national organization of the modern world. The Palestinian people likewise deserve a state, and Israel ought to participate in its rebirth through recognition and material help if the Palestinians request it. A Jewish theology of liberation is unequivocal in this regard: the Palestinian people have been deeply wronged in the creation of Israel and in the occupation of territories. As we celebrate our empowerment, we must repent our transgressions and stop them immediately. If this is done today, perhaps a hundred years from now we can speak of a confederation of Israel and Palestine and how out of a tragic conflict a healing took place to the benefit of both communities.

A Jewish theology of liberation must also question Jewish empowerment in the United States. As we have seen, the Jewish community looks to the United States to guarantee Israel's security. Rarely is the cost of this guarantee discussed. Too often the *quid pro quo* is unquestioning support of United States military build-up and intervention around the world. Our ethics propel us toward solidarity; our *realpolitik* sees the poor here and in the Third World as threats to a system that is working in our favor. But what if United States militarism and intervention continues and deepens a cycle of poverty for a majority of the world's population? Even liberal statements that emerge from Jewish organizations carry little realistic analysis of the situation. Increasingly vague and rhetorical, the liberal agenda, while important for its time, carries little other than a hope that we will remain undisturbed.[9]

The vague liberal dialogue that now passes for ethical concern continues despite the unethical actions by the State of Israel. We engage in such dialogue in order to protect our own affluence. There is little dispute that Jews have made it in North America, though there are many poor Jews about whom neither Jews nor non-

Jews want to speak. Impoverished Jews are a part of our past that we want to bury, for they remind us of the ghetto we have now escaped. Could we say that, although numerous museum and theatrical celebrations of our recent past abound, we are actually ashamed of our lives lived on the periphery, unnoticed by the general society and unrewarded with money and status?

Norman Podhoretz, a leading Jewish neoconservative, woke up one morning and realized it was better to be rich than poor, better to be powerful than weak. In some ways this has been a collective wakening rather than an individual's inspiration. Few would argue with his general theme unless an alternative was presented: that it is better for all to have access to the goods of life and be empowered to participate equally in the decision-making process in society. However, to reach this goal is to understand how affluence is created and how in its creation others are denied. As defined in our society, power demands the weakness of others and feeds on that weakness. Democracy may be the watchword; oligarchy is the reality. Capitalism, as practiced, may represent affluence for the few; it means unemployment and poverty for many. Most often, as Jews, we are aware of this only dimly, through newspapers and television. But those below us know we are riding the crest of a tidal wave. A Jewish theology of liberation asks that the liberal analysis that supports our affluence be deepened with a liberationist economic and political critique that paradoxically has often been pioneered, nurtured, and expanded by secular Jews on the left.[10]

PRACTICING JUDAISM IN A POST-HOLOCAUST WORLD

A Jewish theology of liberation is also a call to those Jews who have ceased to identify with the Jewish community. In the nineteenth and twentieth centuries, "secular" Jews abandoned or were forced out of the community because of their ideals and activism. Their critique of economic and political power carries forth the Jewish ethical ideal without religious language. Though progressive religious Jews did exist, the critique of religion and capitalism left many with little choice but to break out on their own. Many Jews on the left became a-theistic toward the religion and economy of their day, and it is only now that we can recognize the peculiar paradox they represented: many of those who refused the God of the status quo carried forth in various ways the essential witness of Jewish life, and many of those who prayed fervently adopted the idols of modern life. However, while it is true that some religious Jews actively pursued justice, it is also true that some who broke away adopted new idols, a monolithic secularism, and too often a Stalinist Marxism.

This split, perhaps inevitable for its time, serves little purpose today. The religious Jew needs the secular and socialist critique in order to be more fully Jewish, and the secular Jew benefits from ideals and symbols spoken in a language that has languished. For what is a religious Jew if not one who transforms the world because of his or her faith? And what is a secular Jewish leftist if not a practicing Jew without portfolio? And the division between religious and secular, as well as the possible dialogue, raises an important question that a Jewish theology of liberation cannot shirk: in the midst of Holocaust and empowerment, who indeed is a practicing Jew?

The Holocaust theologians portray a Jew today as one who remembers the Holocaust and participates in the survival and empowerment of the Jewish people. A secondary although important theme is pursuit of the ethical. As we have seen, a Jewish theology of liberation raises the ethical again to a primary status, with the additional dynamic of solidarity and remembrance of paths untaken. Holocaust theologians thus have redefined the notion of practicing Jew from one who engages in ritual and observance of the Law to one who cherishes memory, survival, and empowerment, and a Jewish theology of liberation adds to that definition a critical and efficacious pursuit of justice and peace. Yet most Jews, whether denominationally Orthodox or confirmed secularists, continue to accept the definitions established in a different era. How often do we meet a secular Jew giving his or her life to justice and feeling estranged from "religiosity," and an Orthodox Jew who contributes to injustice and feels self-righteous about his or her "religiosity"? Today we must reevaluate the notion of a practicing Jew if the term itself is to retain any value at all.[11]

We must also assert quite clearly that identification with the State of Israel is not, in and of itself, a religious act. The contrary is also true: the refusal to see the State of Israel as central to Jewish spirituality is not, in and of itself, an offense warranting excommunication. A practicing Jew within the liberationist perspective sees the State of Israel as neither central nor peripheral, but rather as a necessary and flawed attempt to create an autonomous presence within the Middle East. The Jewish people have had a continuous presence in the area for more than five thousand years, and recent history has mandated a return. However, a Jewish liberationist perspective denies that Jewish history revolves around a return to the land and that Israel is *the* important Jewish community. Jewish people live in Israel and thus deserve solidarity with Jews in North America and elsewhere; the reverse is true as well.[12]

The equation of Zionism with Judaism is clearly inappropriate. Zionists are those who have settled in Israel, and even in Israel non-Zionist Jews appear. Those outside of Israel who claim Israel as the center of their Jewish identity are "Israelists" or "Israel-identified" Jews rather than Zionists. Israelis are leaving Israel at a higher rate than Diaspora Jews are emigrating to Israel. Israelis who leave Israel are Israeli-born Jews who live elsewhere; they are no longer Zionists. The great majority of the Jewish people may be Israeli-identified, but by definition they are something other than Zionists. Solidarity with one's own people is hardly exhausted by one's position on the issue of Zionism and Israel, though the framers of the discussion would have us believe this to be the case. So much energy and emotion have been spent on equating Zionism and Judaism that an understandable fear exists when even an adjustment is suggested. But what if Israel as a state ceased to exist, either involuntarily through military force, or voluntarily through confederation with the Palestinian community? Would Judaism and the Jewish people cease to exist, or would the energies of Jewish resistance and hope be rechannelled? The Jewish people existed before the State of Israel and will exist long after the nation-state system ceases to exist.[13]

Necessarily involved with the Jewish people, a practicing Jew is also called to enter into the broader tradition of faith and struggle. Ecumenical dialogue, as defined over the last quarter century, has its importance and its limitations. Many Jews see such dialogue as wasteful and wrong, as if communication will compromise ortho-doxy and the "enemy" will always be the same. Those who reach out in pain and expectancy create an important bridge of under-standing, even of compassion. However, today we have to understand the limitations of ecumenical dialogue and where that dialogue is leading. The broader tradition of faith and struggle is occurring within a context wholly different from traditional Jewish and Christian institutions. Too often these powerbrokers retain power by maintaining the status quo, and this, in return, means maintaining domination and oppression. There is no doubt, also, that the implicit or explicit theology brought to these dialogues from the Jewish side is a Holocaust theology that centers on empowerment and support of Israel. To be in good faith the Christian dialogue partners must first and foremost signal their wholehearted assent, and any vacillation is equated with anti-Semitism. As with the Perlmutters, conversants are chosen or excluded depending on their stance toward Israel. Yet where can this dialogue lead if its main focus is shifted simply from the Christian propensity to seek the conversion of the Jews to the Jewish effort to demand the conversion of Christians to Zionism? What each of us needs instead is a critical partner who repents for past transgressions and is also allowed to think critically. As painful and as paradoxical as it might seem to many, the Jewish community cannot address the question of Israel alone for any length of time: yes-men and -women for partners render little assistance to a community that needs assurance *and* critique. A true Jewish liberationist believes that Palestine and the support of a Palestinian state formed by the Palestine Liberation Organization need to be part of any discussion of Israel and thus part of the ecumenical dialogue.[14]

A Jewish theology of liberation encourages a dialogue with other liberationist theologies and communities in a gesture of humility and solidarity. At this point, the few contacts that have been made are by Jews on the left without Jewish identification or by Jewish institutional leaders and academics who often seek to lecture Christian theologians on their faulty exegetical methods and their revival of Christian triumphalism. The main point seems to be that the Jewish community fears the theological and political change such liberationist perspectives engender. But are we not missing the essential point of their struggle? The point is that they are speaking for those who are suffering. And this should open the way to solidarity between our Jewish community and liberation theologians. Our fear for survival seems to cover over a deeper fear: the discovery that we are less and less in touch with our own witness.

Instead of the affluent and relatively empowered lecturing power-less people on the importance of uncritical support for Israel, perhaps it is time for us to be silent and to listen to the painful, moving, and sometimes contradictory stories that emerge from the underside. By listening instead of lecturing we might find that we are increasingly complicit in their suffering and, at the same time, we might begin to discover paths to solidarity important to them and to us.

A Jewish theology of liberation recognizes that the world has changed and that by simply applying pre-Holocaust and Holocaust categories to the contemporary world we close our eyes and ears to the pain and possibility of the present. By carrying our own history we bequeath insight to contemporary struggles. If we are over-whelmed, though, by history and seek to overwhelm others, our memory becomes a wedge of anger and insularity, a blunt instru-ment rather than a delicately nurtured memory. As Walter Ben-jamin correctly points out, the memory of our enslaved ancestors can either enslave us or set us free. Paradoxically the Exodus paradigm may be enlightening here. For the memories of past slavery may encourage a return to bondage in the guise of freedom, as if a known reality is better than the unknown. Those who sought a return to Egypt were refusing the risk of the wilderness, certainly an understandable position. Yet freedom lay elsewhere, beyond the known, and new patterns of life and worship were to be developed in the pain and struggle of liberation.

As risky and problematic as it is, we are called today to the wilderness; but that call is a promise of liberation. Chastened by history, we can no longer see liberation as the omnipotent preserve of God hovering over us by day and leading us by night, or simply as the search for the empowerment of our own people in North America and Israel. We can ill afford such innocence in the pres-ence of burning children, whether they be in Poland or in Lebanon. As people in perpetual exile from Jerusalem, a status that formed the heart of our prayerful lamentations, we return today to form our prayers for a new generation of exiles that we have created. The celebration of our Exodus from Egypt, the Passover, again con-tains lessons: we mourn the loss of Egyptian blood shed for our liberation and are cautioned on our most festive holiday to recall the strangers in our own midst, for we were once strangers in a strange land. The *Haggadah* also asks us to go one step farther, to imagine ourselves in slavery. The celebration of freedom is thus disturbed by our own bondage. The warning is twofold: empowerment is covered with blood, and even the oppressors' blood is lamented; and empowerment with its rationale and justification is always confronted with forms of bondage into which we are tempted to enter. Empowerment is neither final nor univocal: it is a stage toward a solidarity with self and others and contains its own critique, fashioned not by the victors but by the slaves in history and slaves today. It is understandable that we often confuse empowerment with liberation because empowerment is convenient and self-serving. As we have also seen, however, empowerment of one people can force others into exile.

The voices of critique and renewal within empowerment—those willing to enter the night and create bonds of solidarity—walk the path of liberation within the Jewish community today, though they are often uncelebrated and unrecognized. As in other communities, the path of liberation is lightly traveled, and the great majority carry on as if the victors have the final word. That the victims, once empowered, behave like the victors they once rebelled against is a sad, but not unique, fact of history. That the security of the victors is one step from the anguish of the victims is rarely understood, even when the victors have recently emerged from the fires. There is cynicism in both power and despair, and perhaps the two are linked in a cycle from which it is impossible to escape. The exilic voices, then, represent an idealism that many feel is best left on the periphery.

The hope of liberation, however, remains always before us, and five thousand years of history, with its chapters of Holocaust and empowerment, provide a unique foundation upon which to build a future. The prophetic, like faith itself, ebbs and flows, waiting to be rediscovered by the people who bequeathed it to the world. The new urgency, represented by the "burning children" of all peoples, calls us to this rediscovery with a bewildering urgency. As much as any time in history, the world needs this witness, and at the crossroads of our own history, so do we. A Jewish theology of liberation seeks to join with others in rediscovering the prophetic voice with the hope that we can become what we are called to be.

AFTERWORD

The Palestinian Uprising and the Future of the Jewish People

Since December 1987, as the twenty-year occupation of the West Bank and Gaza erupted into a veritable civil war, the Jewish community in North America and Israel awakened with a start. An outpouring of anger ensued over the betrayal of our ethical witness and a commitment arose to end the occupation. Michael Lerner, editor of the progressive Jewish journal *Tikkun,* summed up these feelings with an editorial titled, "The Occupation: Immoral and Stupid." In passionate and unequivocal language he called on Israel to "Stop the beatings, stop the breaking of bones, stop the late night raids on people's homes, stop the use of food as a weapon of war, stop pretending that you can respond to an entire people's agony with guns and blows and power. Publicly acknowledge that the Palestinians have the same right to national self-determination that we Jews have and negotiate a solution with representatives of the Palestinians!"[1]

In a sense, Lerner and many other Jews are moving toward a position almost unthinkable before the Palestinian uprising: solidarity with the Palestinian people. For the uprising brings again to mind Johann Baptist Metz's reflection, previously quoted, on the Christian and Jewish journey after the Holocaust. The statement bears repetition: "We Christians can never go back behind Auschwitz: to go beyond Auschwitz, if we see clearly, is impossible for us by ourselves. It is possible only together with the victims of

123

Auschwitz." In light of the uprising, these words assume a new meaning, relating to the common journey of Jew and Palestinian. For Jews the challenge might be stated thusly: "We Jews can never go back behind empowerment: to go beyond empowerment, if we see clearly, is impossible for us by ourselves. It is possible only with the victims of our empowerment."[2]

Thus the question facing the Jewish people in Israel and around the world involves, and yet moves far beyond, negotiation of borders, recognition of the P.L.O., the cessation of the expropriation of human, land and water resources in the occupied territories, and even the public confession of Israeli torture and murder. For in the end the Israeli-Palestinian conflict involves the political, military and economic spheres of Jewish life while at the same time addressing the deepest theological presuppositions of post-Holocaust Jewry. Without addressing the implicit and explicit theology of our community, any adjustment of political, military, or economic borders will represent superficial moments to be transgressed when the opportunity presents itself. Surely political settlement of any significance in Israel and Palestine without a movement toward solidarity is, by the very nature of the conflict, impossible.

As the uprising has made clear, the normative theology of the Jewish community today—Holocaust theology—is unable to articulate this path of solidarity. Nor can the most well known of Jewish spokespersons, some of whom helped to create this theology and others who operate within it, speak clearly on this most important issue. There are many reasons for this inability to address concisely the subject of solidarity. Holocaust theology, emerging out of reflection on the death camps, represents the Jewish people as we were, helpless and suffering; it does not and cannot speak of the people we are today and who we are becoming—powerful and often oppressive. Holocaust theology argues correctly for the Jewish need to be empowered; it lacks the framework and the skills of analysis to investigate the cost of that empowerment. Holocaust theology speaks eloquently about the struggle for human dignity in the death camps, and radically about the question of God and Jewish survival, but has virtually nothing to say about the ethics of a Jewish state possessing nuclear weapons, supplying military arms and assistance to authoritarian regimes, expropriating land and torturing resisters to Israeli occupation.[3]

Although this information is readily available and accepted as documented by the world community, written about or even discovered by Jews in Israel and in the United States, Holocaust theologians often refuse to accept it, as if the suggestion that Jews could support such policies, rather than the policies themselves, is treasonable and grounds for excommunication from the community. Because of the power of Holocaust theology in mainstream Jewish institutions, media and organized Jewish religious life, these "facts" are deemed outside of Jewish discourse *as if they are not happening, because it is impossible that Jews would do such things.* Thus a community which prides itself on its intelligence and knowledge is on its most crucial issue—the behavior of our people—profoundly ignorant.[4]

That is why the dialectic of Holocaust and empowerment, surfaced in Holocaust theology, needs, more than ever, to be confronted by the dynamic and dangerous element of solidarity. Solidarity, often seen as a reaching out to other communities in a gesture of good will, at the same time necessitates a probing of one's own community. To come into solidarity, knowledge of the other is needed; soon, though, we understand a deeper knowledge of self is called for as well. If we recognize the national aspirations of the Palestinian people, that is only a step toward the more difficult and critical question of how Israeli policy has interacted with those aspirations. If we support the struggle of South African blacks, the relationship of Israel and the South African government needs a thorough and continuing investigation. What we find today is a powerful and flawed Jewish community which has become something other than that innocent victim abandoned by the world.[5]

Because of the Palestinian uprising, increasing numbers of Jews are beginning to understand that our historical situation has changed radically in the last two decades and that something terrible, almost tragic, is happening to us. With what words do we speak such anguished sentiments? Do we feel alone with these feelings so that they are better left unspoken? Do such words, once spoken, condemn us as traitors or with the epithet, self-hating Jew? Or does articulating the unspeakable challenge the community to break through the silence and paralysis which threatens to engulf us? And those of us who know and empathize with the Palestinians, can we speak without being accused of creating the context for another holocaust? Can we be seen as emissaries of an option to halt the cycle of destruction and death?[6]

This is the challenge which faces the Jewish people. And with it is the task of creating a new Jewish theology consonant with the history we are creating and the history we want to bequeath to our children. When all is said and done, should it be that we are powerful where once we were weak, that we are invincible where once we were vulnerable? Or would we rather be able to say that the power we created, necessary and flawed, was simply a tool to move beyond empowerment to a liberation that encompassed all those struggling for justice, including those we once knew as enemy? And that our power, used in solidarity with others, brought forth a healing in the world which ultimately began to heal us of our wounds from over the millennia?

New movements of renewal within the Jewish community which have developed or expanded during the uprising point the way to this theology. In Israel, the Committee Confronting the Iron Fist, made up of Israelis and Palestinians whose first publication carried the provocative title "We Will Be Free In Our Own Homeland!" creates dialogue situations and stages demonstrations to end the occupation. Members of the anti-war movement *Yesh Gvul,* or There Is A Limit, made up of Israelis who refused to serve in the Lebanese War and today refuse to serve in the West Bank and Gaza, are courageous in their willingness to say "no" to the oppression of others, even at the expense of imprisonment. Women in Black, made up of Israelis who vigil in mourning dress, and Women Against Occupation, who adopt Palestinian women political prisoners and detainees, are just two more of many Jewish groups protesting the occupation and expressing solidarity with the Palestinian uprising.[7]

Since the uprising North American Jews are increasingly vocal in relation to the pursuit of justice in the Middle East. New Jewish Agenda, a movement of secular and religious Jews, continues to argue for Israeli security and the just demands of Palestinian nationhood. *Tikkun,* the progressive Jewish magazine, is in the forefront of vocal argument and organizing for a new understanding of the Israeli-Palestinian situation. And now with the recent crisis, Jewish intellectuals, such as Arthur Hertzberg and Irving Howe, and institutions, including the Union of American Hebrew

Congregations, have voiced their horror at Israeli policies in the occupied territories.[8]

What these individuals and movements represent is a groping toward a theological framework which nurtures rather than hinders expressions of solidarity. It is almost as if a long-repressed unease is coming to the surface, breaking through the language and symbol once deemed appropriate. Of course the risk is that if the crisis passes without fundamental change, the language of solidarity will recede and the more familiar patterns will reassert themselves. And it is true to state that even the movements cited are often limited in their scope and vision, equivocating where necessary to retain some credibility within the Jewish community.

Still the drift is unmistakable and the task clear. The theological framework we need to create is hardly a departure, but a renewal of the themes which lie at the heart of our tradition, the exodus and the prophetic, interpreted in the contemporary world. A Jewish theology of liberation is our oldest theology, our great gift to the world, which has atrophied time and again only to be rediscovered by our own community and other communities around the world. A Jewish theology of liberation confronts Holocaust and empowerment with the dynamic of solidarity, providing a bridge to others as it critiques our own abuses of power. By linking us to all those who struggle for justice, a Jewish theology of liberation will, in the long run, decrease our sense of isolation and abandonment and thus begin a process of healing so necessary to the future of the Jewish community.

If it is true that we cannot go back behind empowerment, we now know that we cannot go forward alone. Could it be that the faces which confront us are those of the Palestinian people and that somehow in these faces lies the future of the Jewish people? This is why a two state solution is only the beginning of a long and involved process that demands political compromise and a theological transformation which is difficult to envision. For if our theology is not confronted and transformed, then the political solutions will be superficial and transitory. A political solution may give impetus to this theological task; a theological movement may nurture a political solution. However, a political solution without a theological transformation simply enshrines the tragedy to be repeated again.

Here we enter the most difficult of arenas; for the presupposition is that in the faces of the Palestinians lies the future of what it means to be Jewish, that at the center of the struggle to be faithful as a Jew today is the suffering and liberation of the Palestinian people. Despite the uprising, such a thought is still *hardly considered in Jewish theological circles.* At some point, though, an essential integration of Jew and Palestinian in a larger arena of political, cultural and religious life is integral to a Jewish future. But this assumes that a fundamental confession and repentance of past and present transgressions is possible and a critical understanding of our history uncovered.

THE OCCUPATION IS OVER

Since the beginning of the uprising we have awakened to reports of beatings and the deaths of Palestinian people, mostly youth, in the occupied territories. But this raises a strange and disturbing question: if Palestinians cease to die, will the uprising—at least for North American Jews and Christians—cease to matter? A horrible thought follows: for the Palestinian cause it is crucial that they continue to die in ever increasing numbers if we are to understand that *the occupation, as we have known it, is over.* Unable to accept this conclusion, I approached Palestinians and church workers who have returned from the West Bank and Gaza. All have the same thoughts. It is true, and the Palestinian leadership—as well as the Palestinian villagers—understand this tragic fact: the uprising is dependent on the continuing death of children.

But can Jewish Israelis continue to beat and kill Palestinian children *ad infinitum?* Can North American Jews continue to support these horrible acts? And can Christians, especially those who have chosen to repent the anti-Jewishness of the Christian past and who have accepted Israel as an integral part of the contemporary Jewish experience, remain silent on the uprising and Israeli brutality? Or, are we all hoping that somehow the situation will dissipate, go unreported, or better still, disappear? This much seems clear: the willingness of Palestinians to endure torture and death, and the willingness of Israel to inflict such acts of brutality, point to the most difficult of situations which many would choose to ignore—that some basic themes of post-Holocaust Jewish and

Christian life are being exposed in a radical and unrelenting way.

If it is true that the occupation of the territories is in fact over, that it has moved beyond occupation to uprising and civil war, then the theological support for the occupation in Jewish and Christian theology must end as well. The focus of both theologies in their uncritical support of Israel has been shattered. The uprising, therefore, is a crisis on many fronts and is at its deepest level a theological crisis. Of course, like any crisis the uprising presents us with both tragedy and possibility. By uplifting the truth at the price of broken bones and lives, the children of Palestine force us to think again and to break through ignorance, half-truths, and lies. But will we have the tenacity and courage in safe and comfortable North America that the Palestinian children have on the streets of Gaza and the West Bank? Or, will the inevitable allegations of Jewish self-hate and Christian anti-Jewishness deter us? Are we willing to reexamine our theological presuppositions as particular communities and in dialogue with each other, or will we attempt to pass over the question in silence?

It is not too much to say that the uprising poses the future of Judaism in stark and unremitting terms. The tragedy of the Holocaust is well documented and indelibly ingrained in our consciousness: we know who we were. But do we know who we have become? Contemporary Jewish theology helps us come to grips with our suffering; it hardly recognizes that today we are powerful. A theology that holds in tension Holocaust and empowerment speaks eloquently for the victims of Treblinka and Auschwitz yet ignores Sabra and Shatila. It pays tribute to the Warsaw Ghetto uprising but has no place for the uprising of ghetto dwellers on the other side of Israeli power. Jewish theologians insist that the torture and murders of Jewish children be lamented and commemorated in Jewish ritual and belief. It has yet to imagine, though, the possibility that Jews have in turn tortured and murdered Palestinian children. Holocaust theology relates the story of the Jewish people in its beauty and suffering. Yet it fails to integrate the contemporary history of the Palestinian people as integral to our own. Thus, this theology articulates who we were but no longer helps us understand who we have become.

So Jews who are trying to understand the present become a contradiction to themselves while others simply refuse to acknowledge the facts of contemporary Jewish life. A dilemma arises: awareness of Jewish transgressions has no framework to be articulated and acted upon; ignorance (albeit preferred rather than absolute) insists that what is occurring is impossible, that torture and murder are not in fact happening at all, that Jews could not do such things. Jews who become aware have few places to turn theologically, and the ignorant become more and more bellicose in their insistence and in their anger. Meanwhile, despite increasing dissent, Holocaust theology continues as normative in the Jewish community, warning dissident Jews that they approach the terrain of excommunication and continuing to reenforce the ignorance of many Jews as a theological prerequisite to community membership.

As we become more and more powerful, the neoconservative trend is buttressed by fear, anger, and by a deepening sense of isolation. Anyone who works in the Jewish community recognizes this immediately, the almost uncontrollable emotional level that criticism of Israel engenders. To be accused of creating the context for another holocaust is almost commonplace, as are the charges of treason and self-hate. Yet on a deeper level one senses a community which, having emerged from the death camps, sees little option but to fight to the bitter end. It is as if the entire world is still against us, as if the next trains depart for Eastern Europe, as if the death camps remain ready to receive us after an interval of almost half a century. This is why though the entire world understands Yasir Arafat to be a moderate, there is no other name linked by the Jewish community so closely to Adolf Hitler. This is why Prime Minister Shamir spoke of the plans to launch a ship of Palestinian refugees to Israel as an attempt to undermine the state of Israel, as an act of war.[9]

Years after the liberation of the camps, Elie Wiesel wrote, "Were hatred a solution, the survivors, when they came out of the camps, would have had to burn down the whole world." Surely with the nuclear capacity of Israel, coupled with the sense of isolation and anger, Wiesel's statement remains a hope rather than a concluded option. Is it too much to say that any theology which does not understand the absolute difference between the Warsaw Ghetto and Tel Aviv, between Hitler and Arafat, is a theology which may legitimate that which Wiesel cautioned against?

Christians who have entered into solidarity with the Jewish people are similarly in a dilemma. The road to solidarity has been paved both by Christian renewal, especially with regard to the Hebrew scriptures, and by Holocaust theology. Understanding the beauty and suffering of the Jewish people as a call to Christian repentance and transformation hardly prepares the community for a confrontation with Israeli power. How do Christians respond now when, over the years, the centrality of Israel has been stressed as necessary to Christian confession in the arena of dialogue, and no words of criticism against Israel are countenanced as anything but anti-Jewish? Too, Christian Zionism, fundamentalist and liberal, is ever present. What framework do Christians have to probe the history of the state of Israel, to understand the uprising—to question the cost of Jewish empowerment? Can Christian theologians articulate a solidarity with the Jewish people which is a critical solidarity, one that recognizes the suffering *and* the power of the Jewish people? Can Christian theologies in the spirit of a critical solidarity open themselves to the suffering of the Palestinian people as a legitimate imperative of what it means to be Christian today?

The uprising continues to push Christian theologians to rethink their theology and move beyond frightened silence or paternalistic embrace. A critical solidarity is increasingly called for, especially in the works of feminist theologian Rosemary Radford Ruether. As a friend of the Jewish people, Ruether is calling attention to attitudes and behavior which can only lead to disaster. Repentance of Christian anti-Jewishness and the promotion of Jewish empowerment can only be authentic today within the context of a recognition of the legitimate rights of the Palestinian people.[10]

Clearly the Palestinian struggle for nationhood poses more than the prospect of political negotiation and compromise. For Jews and Christians it presents fundamental theological material which lends depth to the inevitable (though long suffering) political solutions. Without this theological component a political solution may or may not appear. However, the lessons of the conflict would surely be lost and thus the political solution would tend toward superficiality and immediacy rather than depth and longevity. A political solution without a theological transformation would simply enshrine the tragedy to be repeated again. An important opportunity to move beyond our present theologies toward theologies of solidarity, which may usher in a new age of ecumenical cooperation, would be lost. Could it be that the struggle of the Palestinian people—their struggle to be faithful—is a key to the Jewish and Christian struggle to be faithful in the contemporary world?

The torture and death of Palestinian children calls us to a theology which recognizes empowerment as a necessary and flawed journey toward liberation. It reminds us that power in and of itself, even for survival, ends in tragedy without the guidance of ethics and a strong sense of solidarity with all those who are struggling for justice. Today, the Palestinian people ask the fundamental question relating to Jewish empowerment: can the Jewish people in Israel, indeed Jews around the world, be liberated without the liberation of the Palestinian people? Once having understood the question posed by the Palestinian people, the occupation can no longer continue. What remains is to build a theological framework which delegitimates the torture and the killing—a theology of liberation which sees solidarity as the essence of what it means to be Jewish and Christian.

A NEW THEOLOGICAL FRAMEWORK

The development of a theological framework is crucial to delegitimate torture and murder—that is, to end theologies which promote a myriad of occupations including, though not limited to, that of the Palestinian people. In this case we focus on the Israeli occupation as the breakthrough point for Jewish theology. The theological framework which legitimates occupation also, if we look closely, forces Jews to take positions on other issues which would be questioned, even abhorred, if the framework were different. If our theology did not support the occupation, its vision of justice and peace would be transformed. Thus we turn again to the prospect that the uprising represents a culmination and a possibility, if we will only seize the moment.

An essential task of Jewish theology is to deabsolutize the state of Israel. To see Israel as an important Jewish community among other Jewish communities, with an historical founding and evolution, is to legitimate theologically what the Jewish people have acted out with their lives: the continuation of diverse Jewish communities outside the state. Thus the redemptive aspect of Jewish survival after the Holocaust is found in a much broader arena than the state of Israel, and must be critically addressed rather than simply asserted in unquestioning allegiance to a state where most Jews do not live. Deabsolutizing Israel hardly means its abandonment. Instead it calls forth a new, more mature relationship. Jews cannot bilocate forever and the strain of defending policies implemented by others, of criticizing without being able to influence directly, of supporting financially and being made to feel guilty for not living in Israel, is impossible to continue over a long period of time. With this new understanding responsibilities between Jewish communities assume a mutuality which includes a critical awareness of the centrality of our ethical tradition as the future of our community. Therefore, the present crisis and any future crisis moves beyond the call for unquestioned allegiance or disassociation from Israel to a critical solidarity with responsibilities and obligations on all sides.[11]

A second parallel task is to deal with the Holocaust in its historical context and to cease its application as a possible future outcome to issues of contemporary Jewish life. The constant use of the Holocaust with reference to Israel is to misjudge and therefore refuse to understand the totally different situation of pre-and post-Holocaust Jewry. Pre-Holocaust European Jewry had no state or military; it was truly defenseless before the Nazi onslaught. Israel is a state with superior military ability. Pre-Holocaust European Jewry lived among populations whose attitudes toward Jews varied from tolerance to hatred. Post-Holocaust Jewry, with its population concentrations in France, England, Canada, and the United States, resides in countries where anti-Jewishness is sporadic and politically inconsequential. Pre-Holocaust Jewry lived among Christians who had as a group little reason to question Christian anti-Jewishness. Post-Holocaust Jewry lives among Christians who have made repeated public statements, writings, even ritual affirmations of the centrality of the Jewish people and Christian culpability for an anti-Jewish past. The differences between pre-and post-Holocaust Jewry can be listed on many other levels as well, which is not to deny that anti-Jewishness continues to exist. As many Jewish writers have pointed out, the paradox is that the most dangerous place for Jews to live today is in the state of Israel rather than the Jewish centers of Europe and North America.

Even in relation to Israel the application of Holocaust language is clearly inappropriate. Israel has been involved in two wars since 1967 and can claim victory in neither; no civilian life was lost outside the battlefield. The great fear, repeated over and over again, is that one day Israel will lose a war and that the civilian population will be annihilated, i.e., another holocaust. It is important to note here that if the situation continues as it is today it is inevitable that one day Israel will lose a war and face the possibility of annihilation. No nation is invincible forever, no empire exists that is not destined to disappear, no country that does not, at some point in its history, lose badly and suffer immensely. Can our present theology exempt Israel from the reality of shifting alliances, military strategies, and political life? *The only way to prevent military defeat is to make peace when you are powerful.* Of course, even here there is never any absolute protection from military defeat, as there is never any absolute protection from persecution. But if military defeat does come and if the civilian population is attacked, the result, though tragic, will not by any meaningful definition be another holocaust. And it would not, by any means, signal the end of the Jewish people, as many Holocaust theologians continue to speculate. It would be a terrible event, too horrible to mention. And perhaps the differences between the Holocaust and any future military defeat of Israel are too obvious to explore, and would hardly need exploration if our present theology was not confused on this most important point.

To deabsolutize the state of Israel and distinguish the historical event of the Holocaust from the situation of contemporary Jewish life is imperative to the third task of Jewish theology: the redefinition of Jewish identity. This is an incredibly difficult and complex task whose parameters can only be touched upon here. Yet it is the most crucial of areas raising the essential question that each generation faces: what does it mean to be Jewish in the contemporary world?

There is little question that Holocaust theology is the normative theology of the Jewish community today and that at the center of this theology is the Holocaust and the state of Israel. Rabbinic theology, the normative Jewish theology for almost two millennia, initially sought to continue as if neither the Holocaust nor the state of Israel were central to the Jewish people, and Reform Judaism, the interesting, sometimes shallow nineteenth-century attempt to come to grips with modern life, also sought to bypass the formative events of our time. Yet after the Holocaust, and especially since the 1967 Six Day War, both theological structures have been transformed with an underlying Holocaust theology. Secular Jews, as well, often affiliated with progressive politics and economics, have likewise experienced a shifting framework of interpretation. Though not explicitly religious, their aid has been solicited by Holocaust theologians to build the state of Israel as the essential aspect of belonging to the Jewish people. In sum, both those who believed in Jewish particularity and those who sought a more universal identification have increasingly derived their Jewish identity from the framework of Holocaust and Israel. And there is little reason to believe that any of these frameworks—Orthodox, Reform, or secular humanism—can ever again return to their pre-Holocaust, pre-Israel positions.

We can only move ahead by affirming the place of Holocaust and Israel as important parts of Jewish identity while insisting that they are not and cannot become the sum total of what it means to be Jewish. The point here is to take the dynamic of Holocaust and Israel and understand it in new ways. In both events there is, among other things, an underlying theme of solidarity which has been buried in our anger and isolation. This includes solidarity with our own people as well as others who have come into solidarity with us. As importantly, if we recover our own history, there is a theme of Jewish solidarity with others even in times of great danger. The latter include some of the early settlers and intellectuals involved in the renewal of the Jewish community in Palestine, well-known figures like Albert Einstein, Hannah Arendt, and many others.[12]

Even during the Holocaust there were voices, Etty Hillesum, for one, who argued that their suffering should give birth to a world of mutuality and solidarity so that no people should ever suffer again. As she voluntarily accompanied her people to Auschwitz, Hillesum was hardly a person who went like a lamb to her slaughter. Rather, she chose a destiny as an act of solidarity with her own people and the world. Is it possible that those who affirmed human dignity where it was most difficult—and those who argued, and continue to argue today, for reconciliation with the Palestinian people even with the risks involved—represent the only future worth bequeathing to our children? By emphasizing our dignity and solidarity we appropriate the event of Holocaust and Israel as formative in a positive and critical way. Thus they ask us to once again embrace the world with the hope that our survival is transformative for our own people and the world.

The key to a new Jewish identity remains problematic unless we understand that deabsolutizing Israel, differentiating Holocaust and the contemporary Jewish situation, and recovering the history of solidarity within our tradition and with those outside it, leads us to a critical confrontation with our own empowerment. To celebrate our survival is important; to realize that our empowerment has come at a great cost is another thing altogether. Can we, at the fortieth anniversary of the state of Israel, realize that the present political and religious sensibilities can only lead to disaster? Can we argue openly that the issue of empowerment is much broader than an exclusive Jewish state and that other options, including autonomy with confederation, may be important to contemplate for the fiftieth anniversary of Israel? Can we openly articulate that as American Jews we can no longer ask American foreign policy to support policies which contradict the ethical heart of what it means to be Jewish? Can we, in good conscience and faith, appeal to Christians, Palestinians, and people of good will around the world to help us end the occupation and if we do not heed the call, to force us to stop for our own sake?

For this is the place we have arrived, well beyond the pledge of loyalty and the private criticism that has abounded for so many years. The uprising challenges the power of the Israeli government and the heart of the Jewish people. But the power to inflict injury and death remains. And therefore the power to change our history, to redefine our inheritance, to alter what it means to be Jewish remains in the hands of those who would see the occupation continue. And with the occupation come a myriad of policies around the world which bring only shame to those who invoke the victims of the Holocaust to legitimate terror.

With the uprising we have lost our innocence; a Jewish theology of liberation must begin with this loss. A weak and helpless people has arisen with a power that surprises and now saddens us. A people set apart returns to the history of nations less as a beacon than as a fellow warrior, living at the expense of others, almost forfeiting its sense of purpose. The commanding voice of Sinai and of Auschwitz beckons us to struggle to reclaim the ethical witness of the Jewish people.

Notes

1. This chapter is an expanded and revised analysis of theology which responds to the Holocaust event. My thoughts on this topic first appeared in "Notes Toward a Jewish Theology of Liberation," *Doing Theology in the United States* 1 (Spring/Summer 1985):5–17.

2. In the Dictrict Court of Jerusalem, criminal case No. 40/61, the Attorney-General of the government of Israel v. Adolph Eichmann. Minutes of Session No. 30, pp. L1, M1, M2, N1.

3. Richard L. Rubenstein, *The Cunning of History: Mass Death and the American Future* (New York: Harper and Row, 1975), pp. 4–5. Although the long and distressing history of Christian anti-Semitism has been well documented, a brief examination of some of its manifestations, as outlined by Jewish Holocaust historian Raul Hilberg, is illuminating. In his monumental work *The Destruction of the European Jews* (New York: Harper and Row, 1961), Hilberg displays the similarities between the early and medieval Church law and Nazi legislation.

Canon Law	Nazi Measure
Prohibition of intermarriage and of sexual intercourse between Christians and Jews, Synod of Elvira, 306	Law for the Protection of German Blood and Honor, September 15, 1935 (RGB1, I, 1146.)
Jews and Christians not permitted to eat together, Synod of Elvira, 306	Jews barred from dining cars (Transport Minister to Interior Minister, December 30, 1939, Document NG-3995.)
Jews not allowed to hold public office, Synod of Clermont, 535	Law for the Re-establishment of the Professional Civil Service, April 7, 1933 (RGB1 I, 175.)

Jews not allowed to employ Christian servants or possess Christian slaves, 3d Synod of Orleans, 538

Law for the Protection of German Blood and Honor, September 15, 1935 (RGB1, I, 1146.)

Jews not permitted to show themselves in the streets during Passion Week, 3d Synod of Orleans, 538

Decree authorizing local authorities to bar Jews from the streets on certain days (i.e., Nazi holidays), December 3, 1938 (RGB1 I, 1676.)

Burning of the Talmud and other books, 12th Synod of Toledo, 681

Book burnings in Nazi Germany

Christians not permitted to patronize Jewish doctors, Trulanic Synod, 692

Decree of July 25, 1938 (RGB1 I, 969.)

Christians not permitted to live in Jewish homes, Synod of Narbonne, 1050

Directive by Göring providing for concentration of Jews in houses, December 28, 1938 (Bormann to Rosenberg, January 17, 1939, PS-69.)

Jews obliged to pay taxes for support of the Church to the same extent as Christians, Synod of Gerona, 1078

The "Sozialaugleichsabgabe" which provided that Jews pay a special income tax in lieu of donations for Party purposes imposed on Nazis, December 24, 1940 (RGB1 I, 1666.)

Jews not permitted to be plaintiffs or witnesses against Christians in the Courts, 3d Lateran Council, 1179, Canon 26

Proposal by the Party Chancellery that Jews not be permitted to institute civil suits, September 9, 1942 (Bormann to Justice Ministry, September 9, 1942, NG-151.)

Jews not permitted to withhold inheritance from descendants who had accepted Christianity, 3d Lateran Council, 1179, Canon 26

Decree empowering the Justice Ministry to void wills offending the "sound judgment of the people," July 31, 1938 (RGB1 I, 937.)

The marking of Jewish clothes with a badge, 4th Lateran Council 1215, Canon 68 (Copied from the legislation by Caliph Omar II (634–44),

Decree of September 1, 1941 (RGB1 I, 547.)

who had decreed that Christians
wear blue belts and Jews, yellow
belts.)

Construction of new synagogues prohibited, Council of Oxford, 1222	Destruction of synagogues in entire Reich, November 10, 1938 (Heydrich to Göring, November 11, 1938, PS-3058.)
Compulsory ghettos, Synod of Breslau, 1267	Order by Heydrich, September 21, 1939 (PS-3363.)
Jews not permitted to obtain academic degrees, Council of Basel, 1434, Session XIX	Law against Overcrowding of German Schools and Universities, April 25, 1933 (RGB1 I, 225) (pp. 5–6).

Anti-Semitism, however, was not restricted to the Roman Catholic church during this period; it also permeated the thoughts and teachings of the Protestant Reformers. This is most clearly evident in the writings of Martin Luther. In his book *About the Jews and Their Lies,* Luther sketched the main outlines of what later became the Nazi portrait of the Jewish people. "Herewith you can readily see how they understand and obey the fifth commandment of God, namely, that they are thirsty bloodhounds and murderers of all Christendom, with full intent, now for more than fourteen hundred years, and indeed they were often burned to death upon the accusation that they had poisoned water and wells, stolen children, and torn and hacked them apart, in order to cool their temper secretly with Christian blood. . . . Now see what a fine, thick, fat lie that is when they complain that they are held captive by us. It is more than fourteen hundred years since Jerusalem was destroyed, and at this time it is almost three hundred years since we Christians have been tortured and persecuted by the Jews all over the world (as pointed out above), so that we might well complain that they had now captured us and killed us—which is the open truth. Moreover, we do not know to this day which devil has brought them here into our country; we did not look for them in Jerusalem" (Quoted by Hilberg, p. 9). Luther's portrait of the Jews as wanting to rule the world, as arch-criminals, killers of Christ and of all Christendom and as plague, pestilence, and pure misfortune was inherited by the Nazis. Thus for Hilberg the Nazi persecution of the Jews should be seen in continuity with Christian persecution, a continuity the Nazis brought to logical conclusion. According to Hilberg, there have been three anti-

Jewish policies since the fourth century of the Common Era: conversion, expulsion, and annihilation. "The missionaries of Christianity," Hilberg writes, "had said in effect: You have no right to live among us as Jews. The secular rulers who followed had proclaimed: You have no right to live among us. The German Nazis at last decreed: You have no right to live" (pp. 3–4). Hilberg continues, "The process began with the attempt to drive Jews into Christianity. The development was continued in order to force the victims into exile. It was finished when the Jews were driven to their deaths. The German Nazis, then, did not discard the past; they built upon it. They did not begin a development; they completed it" (p. 4).

    4. Irving Abella and Harold Troper, *None Is Too Many* (Toronto: Lester and Orpen Dennys, 1983), p. v. After discussing the terrible record of England, Argentina, Brazil, Australia, and the United States with regard to Jewish refugees, the authors relate, "As for Canada: between 1933 and 1945 Canada found room within her borders for fewer than 5,000 Jews; after the war, until the founding of Israel in 1948, she admitted but 8,000 more. That record is arguably the worst of all refugee-receiving states" (p. vi). For the response of the United States see David S. Wyman, *The Abandonment of the Jews: America and the Holocaust 1941–1945* (New York: Pantheon, 1984).

    5. Alexander Donat, *The Holocaust Kingdom: A Memoir* (New York: Rinehart, 1965), p. 9.

    6. Elie Wiesel, *A Jew Today* (New York: Random House, 1978), p. 11.

    7. Ibid., p. 18.

    8. Elie Wiesel, *Night,* trans. Stella Rodway (New York: Avon, 1969), p. 44.

    9. Robert McAfee Brown, *Elie Wiesel: Messenger to All Humanity* (Notre Dame: University of Notre Dame Press, 1983), p. 54. Wiesel, *Night,* p. 78.

    10. Wiesel, *Night,* p. 76.

    11. Elie Wiesel, *Dimensions of the Holocaust* (Evanston, Illinois: Northwestern University Press, 1977), p. 16.

    12. Elie Wiesel, *The Gates of the Forest* (New York: Avon, 1967), pp. 6–9.

    13. Rubenstein, *Cunning of History,* pp. 68–77. Also see Rubenstein's *After Auschwitz: Radical Theology and Contemporary Judaism* (New York: Bobbs-Merrill, 1966).

    14. Ibid., pp. 70–71.

    15. Ibid., pp. 71–73. For a detailed study of Jewish leadership during this difficult time, see Isaiah Trunk, *Judenrat: The Jewish Councils in Eastern Europe Under Nazi Occupation* (New York: Stein and Day, 1977).

    16. Ibid., p. 2.

    17. Ibid., pp. 2, 92–94.

18. Ibid., p. 91. Rubenstein writes: "Does not the Holocaust demonstrate that there are absolutely no limits to the degradation and assault the managers and technicians of violence can inflict upon men and women who lack the power of effective resistance? If there is a law that is devoid of all penalty when violated, does it have any functional significance in terms of human behavior? . . . We are sadly forced to conclude that we live in a world that is *functionally* godless and that human rights and dignity depend upon the power of one's community to grant or withhold them from its members" (pp. 90, 91).

19. Emil Fackenheim, *God's Presence in History: Jewish Affirmations and Philosophical Reflections* (New York: New York University Press, 1970), p. 81.

20. Ibid., p. 84. Also see p. 87. Fackenheim continues: "A Jew is commanded to descend from the cross and, in so doing, not only to reiterate his ancient rejection of an ancient Christian view but also to suspend the time-honored Jewish exaltation of martyrdom. For after Auschwitz, Jewish life is more sacred than Jewish death, were it even for the sanctification of the divine name. The left-wing secularist Israeli journalist Amos Kenan writes: 'After the death camps, we are left only one supreme value: Existence' " (p. 87).

21. Emil Fackenheim, *To Mend the World: Foundations of Future Jewish Thought* (New York: Schocken Books, 1982), p. 25; Pelagia Lewinska, cited there, pp. 25, 26. For a more detailed sense of the struggle to be faithful within the Holocaust world, see Marc H. Ellis, *Faithfulness in an Age of Holocaust* (Amity, New York: Amity House, 1986).

22. Fackenheim, *God's Presence,* p. 86. Also see Fackenheim, *Mend the World.*

23. Irving Greenberg, "Cloud of Smoke, Pillar of Fire: Judaism, Christianity and Modernity After the Holocaust," in *Auschwitz: Beginning of a New Era?* ed. Eva Fleischner (New York: KTAV, 1977), pp. 9–19.

24. Ibid., pp. 28, 29. Greenberg continues: "Modernity fostered the excessive rationalism and utilitarian relations which created the need for and susceptibility to totalitarian mass movements and the surrender of moral judgement. The secular city sustained the emphasis on value-free sciences and objectivity, which created unparalleled power but weakened its moral limits. . . . In the light of Auschwitz, secular twentieth-century civilization is not worthy of this transfer of our ultimate loyalty" (p. 28).

25. Ibid., p. 27.

26. Ibid., p. 32.

27. Ibid., p. 22.

28. One beautiful example of Christians providing refuge for Jews is found in Philip Hallie, *Lest Innocent Blood Be Shed: The Story of the Village of Chambon and How Goodness Happened There* (New York:

Harper and Row, 1979). Also see Nechama Tec, *When Light Pierced the Darkness: Christian Rescue of Jews in Nazi-Occupied Poland* (New York: Oxford University Press, 1986). The history of those who were not willing to do all that was needed to be done is recorded in John F. Morley, *Vatican Diplomacy and the Jews During the Holocaust 1939-1943* (New York: KTAV, 1980). Rev. Morley writes, "It must be concluded that Vatican diplomacy failed the Jews during the Holocaust by not doing all that it was possible for it to do on their behalf. It also failed itself because in neglecting the needs of the Jews, and pursuing a goal of reserve rather than humanitarian concern, it betrayed the ideals that it had set for itself. The Nuncios, the Secretary of State, and most of all, the Pope share the responsibility for this dual failure" (p. 209).

29. Johann Baptist Metz, *The Emergent Church: The Future of Christianity in a Postbourgeois World,* trans. Peter Mann (New York: Crossroad, 1981), p. 19. As we shall see, this dictum, when applied to Christians and Jews, may provide the path to a new form of solidarity.

CHAPTER 2

1. Irving Greenberg, "The Third Great Cycle in Jewish History," *Perspectives* (New York: National Jewish Resource Center, 1981).

2. Ibid., pp. 3–6.

3. Ibid., p. 6.

4. Ibid., p. 8.

5. Ibid., p. 9.

6. Ibid., p. 15.

7. Ibid., p. 18.

8. Ibid., p. 21.

9. Ibid., pp. 22, 23.

10. Ibid., p. 25.

11. Ibid., pp. 25, 26. As to the use of immoral strategies to achieve moral ends Greenberg writes, "The acceptance of the guilt inherent in such actions calls for people of exceptional emotional range and strong orientation both to absolute norms and relative claims, both to judgement and to mercy." At the same time, Greenberg fears a "morally deadening rearmament" and the possibility of idolatry if Judaism fails to critique even as it affirms the State of Israel (p. 25).

12. Ibid., p. 24.

13. Ibid., pp. 27, 28.

14. Ibid., p. 28. Also see Irving Greenberg, "On the Third Era in Jewish History: Power and Politics," *Perspectives* (New York: National Jewish Resource Center, 1980), pp. 18, 19.

15. Greenberg, "Third Era," p. 6.

16. Irving Greenberg, "Power and Peace," *Perspectives* 1 (December 1985): 3, 5.

17. Greenberg, "Third Cycle," p. 28.

18. Ibid., p. 32

19. Ibid., p. 33.

20. Ibid., p. 40.

21. See Abraham J. Heschel, *The Prophets* (New York: Harper and Row, 1962). Also see Martin Buber, *The Prophetic Faith*, trans. Carlyle Witton-Davies (New York: Harper and Row, 1960).

22. This understanding leads Irving Greenberg, in an essay on the lessons of Ronald Reagan's trip to Bitburg in May 1985, to write: "Overall Ronald Reagan's record in commemorating the Holocaust has been very good. He serves as honorary chairman of the campaign to create a national memorial. He has held commemorations of the Holocaust in the White House and spoken passionately of the need to remember. His support for Israel—the single most powerful Jewish commitment that the Holocaust shall not recur, the haven where most of the survivors built their new lives—is exemplary. Our criticism of this particular callous misjudgment must not be allowed to falsify the total overall picture, which is a good one. And we shall have to work with him again." See Greenberg, "Some Lessons from Bitburg," *Perspectives* (May 1985), p. 4. This parallels Elie Wiesel's analysis of Reagan as a "wise and compassionate man" in relation to commemoration of the Holocaust and to his support of Israel. For Richard Rubenstein's confession that his own analysis of the Holocaust leads him to a conservative position, see *The Cunning of History: Mass Death and the American Future* (New York: Harper and Row, 1975), pp. 95–97.

23. Nathan Perlmutter and Ruth Ann Perlmutter, *The Real Anti-Semitism in America* (New York: Arbor House, 1982), p. 107. For a similar view of the world, see Irving Kristol, "The Political Dilemma of American Jews," *Commentary* 67 (July 1984): 23–29.

24. Ibid., pp. 110–111.

25. Ibid., p. 186.

26. Ibid., pp. 156, 157.

27. Ibid., pp. 170–171. The Holyland Fellowship of Christians and Jews founded by Rabbi Yechiel Eckstein seeks to solidify the bond between Fundamentalist Christians and the Jewish community primarily in relation to Christian support for the State of Israel. Among their endorsers are Ronald Reagan, Jack Kemp, conservative Congressman from New York, Pat Robertson of the Christian Broadcasting Network, and Thomas Dine, Executive Director of AIPAC. See *Holyland Fellowship Bulletin* 1 (February 1986): 1–5.

28. Earl Shorris, *Jews Without Mercy: A Lament* (Garden City, New York: Doubleday, 1982), pp. 57–59.

29. Ibid., pp. 12-15.

30. Ibid., p. 60.

31. Roberta Strauss Feuerlicht, *The Fate of the Jews: A People Torn Between Israeli Power and Jewish Ethics* (New York: Times Books, 1983), p. 5.

32. Ibid., pp. 185-87. Feuerlicht writes: "Historically, the relationship between Jew and black in America has not been one of equality. Jews were traders and masters; blacks were merchandise and slaves and servants. In America there is no record of a black who traded in Jews or of a black who owned Jews; I doubt that there are any black housewives who have a Jewish 'girl' come in one day a week to clean. Where blacks were available, neither Jews nor any other whites touched bottom" (pp. 186-87).

33. Ibid., pp. 203-205.

34. Ibid., pp. 220, 245.

35. Ibid., p. 260. Rabbi Balfour Brickner echoes some of these sentiments in relation to the occupation of the West Bank when he writes that "many of us experience a concern that borders on anguish." See Brickner, "The West Bank: Right, Rights and Wrongs," *The Jewish Spectator* (Winter 1983) 48:22-24.

36. Ibid., p. 251. For an Israeli—Palestinian dialogue that seeks to undo this new equation, see Uri Avnery and Hanna Siniora, "A Middle East Peace Is Possible," *The Nation* 242 (April 5, 1986):473, 487-489.

37. Ibid., pp. 258, 259. The casuality figures in the Lebanese War were enormous. Alexander Cockburn writes: "Beginning in the early 1970s Israel systematically bombed Palestinian refugee camps in south Lebanon and Beirut and as far north as Tripoli, killing many thousands. And during the summer of 1982, the Israeli army, conservatively, killed about 19,000 people in Lebanon, mostly Palestinians." See Cockburn "More Swill From Marty," *The Nation* 242 (March 15, 1986), p. 295.

38. Ibid., p. 287.

39. The details and documentation of Israeli involvement in South Africa, Guatemala, El Salvador, and Nicaragua is supplied in Chapter Four.

CHAPTER 3

1. I am indebted to Matthew Lamb for first naming the dialectic of empire and community in a private discussion.

2. Recent books on Jewish renewal include Howard M. Sachar, *Diaspora: An Inquiry into the Contemporary Jewish World* (New York: Harper and Row, 1985) and Charles E. Silberman, *A Certain People: American Jews and Their Lives Today* (New York: Summit Books, 1985). Unfortu-

nately, both of these books reinforce the neoconservative trend in the Jewish community and in fact celebrate it.

3. See Janet Aviad, *Return to Judaism: Religious Renewal in Israel* (Chicago: University of Chicago Press, 1983).

4. Ibid., pp. 1–12.

5. Arthur Waskow's major theological works are *Godwrestling* (New York: Schocken, 1978) and *These Holy Sparks: The Rebirth of the Jewish People* (New York: Harper and Row, 1983).

6. Waskow, *Holy Sparks*, p. 11. As Waskow describes it, he was not alone in his feeling. "All over America, for many different reasons, out of very different biographies, Jews began in those moments of the sixties to regather some sparks. For some it was a moment in 1967 of stark fear for Israel's survival; for others a moment of unutterable joy just a few weeks later, when Jews came to pray again at the Wailing Wall; for others, a moment of revulsion from the America that was lurching toward a genocide in Vietnam; for others, a moment of attraction to Black music or Eastern mysticism or some other life-path richer than that displayed in American mass media. With all, it was a moment of bringing together a spark from the communal Jewish past with a spark from their own person present-growing-toward-a-future. Some need of a growing life—a need for ecstasy or for community, for the grounding whereon to struggle or the breathing space wherein to rest—resonated with a remembered word, a melody, an image from their storehouse of Jewish experience" (p. 14).

7. For the image of "wrestling" see Waskow, *Godwrestling*, pp. 1–22.

8. For Waskow's attempt to place the Holocaust and Israel in the continuity of the Jewish tradition see *Godwrestling*, pp. 128–150. While this is a creative attempt to move the community forward, my own sense is that Greenberg is right and Waskow is wrong: the Holocaust and Israel are events that overpower the Rabbinic tradition.

9. Waskow, *Holy Sparks*, pp. 77–78. For a detailed analysis of the *Chavurah* movement see Bernard Reisman, *The Chavurah: A Contemporary Jewish Experience* (New York: Union of American Hebrew Congregations, 1977).

10. Waskow, *Godwrestling*, pp. 113–116.

11. Ibid., pp. 121, 122.

12. "New Jewish Agenda National Platform," November 28, 1982, p. 1.

13. Excerpts from the Agenda's position statements provide a flavor of the movement: "RACISM—New Jewish Agenda strongly opposes institutional and individual racism. Our ongoing struggle against racism, both within and outside the Jewish community, stems from our own experience of racial bigotry, our traditional commitment to social justice, and our awareness that any division of peoples is harmful to all.

"We are also concerned about the stereotyping and discrimination against Arabs and Arab-Americans that is widespread throughout the United States. The Arab-Israeli conflict does not oblige us to accept this negative view of Arabs and Islam.

"LESBIAN AND GAY JEWS—New Jewish Agenda supports the struggle of Lesbians and Gay Men to lead lives of freedom and dignity. We affirm this at a time when the Right is on the rise and when anti-Gay attacks are increasing. The scapegoating of Lesbians and Gay Men opens the way for the oppression of all minority groups, including Jews. Witness the fact that Lesbians and Gay Men were among the first and most brutally treated victims of the Holocaust.

"ISRAEL, THE PALESTINIANS AND ARAB NEIGHBOURS—After decades of hatred and bloodshed, it is clear that there can be no peace in the Middle East without a political resolution of the conflict among Israelis, Palestinians, and the Arab states. For many Jews, Israel represents the fulfillment of a dream of an independent homeland, and a refuge from centuries of persecution in many lands. The Palestinians have also been exiled, dispersed, denied their rights, and have been kept from establishing political sovereignty in a land of their own. Regardless of how either side views the 'historical legitimacy' of the other, both Israeli Jews and Palestinian Arabs are in the Middle East to stay.

"Our Concern as Jews: As Jews committed to the existence of Israel, we recognize that peace between Israel and its Arab neighbors is essential to Israel's survival. The continuing state of war and military rule over another people diminishes the prospects for Israel's long-term viability. We believe that Israel cannot rule over the Palestinians as an occupying force without degrading the Jewish and human ideals which served as a basis for Israel's creation. A key to the solution of the Arab-Israeli conflict is compromise between Israeli and Palestinian nationalisms. It is not possible to solve this conflict through military means" (Ibid., pp. 3, 4, 6).

14. Jim Statman, "The Jewish Human Rights Delegation to Nicaragua," *Agenda* no. 16 (Winter 1985): 1.

15. Ezra Goldstein, "Jewish Witness for Peace," *Agenda* no. 16 (Winter 1985): 6. Goldstein reported that the relations between Nicaragua and Israel are strained. In a discussion with Herty Lewites, the Minister of Tourism and a Jew, the Minister remarked, "Ten or fifteen thousand people were killed in the revolution by arms and ammunition sold to Somoza by Israel, even after the United States had withdrawn its support. And we are very disturbed at reports that Israel now supplies arms to the Contras" (p. 6).

16. "What Is Oz VeShalom?" *Oz VeShalom English Bulletin*, no. 1 (March 1982): 2.

17. Ibid., p. 2.

18. Yehezkel Landau, ed. *Religious Zionism: Challenges and Choices* (Jerusalem: Oz VeShalom, n.d.), p. 2.

19. "Peace Is to Be Sought and Pursued," *Oz VeShalom English Bulletin*, no. 1 (March 1982): 12, 13.

20. "The Choice is Ours," *Oz VeShalom English Bulletin*, no. 2 (November 1982): 24. In response to the rise of Meir Kahane, an ultra-right-wing movement that seeks to expel the Palestinians from the West Bank, Oz VeShalom handed out leaflets that begin: "KAHANE MANIPULATES YOU! HE TALKS ABOUT THE STATE OF ISRAEL—BUT HE ENDANGERS ITS EXISTENCE: HE TALKS ABOUT THE TORAH OF ISRAEL—BUT HE FALSIFIES JUDAISM: HE PRESENTS EASY 'SOLUTIONS' TO OUR TROUBLES, BUT CONCEALS THE FACTS." See "KAHANE MANIPULATES YOU!," *Oz VeShalom English Bulletin*, no. 6 (Summer 1985): 40. For their opposition to the Lebanese War see "Prayer and Protest in Jerusalem," *Oz VeShalom English Bulletin*, no. 2 (November 1982), pp. 1–7.

21. Phyllis Taylor, "The August Desert Witness," *New Menorah*, second series: no. 4, n.d., p. 5.

22. Alan Mandell, "Prison Witness," ibid., pp. 3, 4, 12; Todd Kaplan, "Pershings into Plowshares," *Menorah* V (September–October 1984): 13.

23. Ibid., pp. 4, 12.

24. Michael Robinson, "On Being Myself—Fully," *Menorah* V (September–October 1984), p. 12.

25. Ibid., p. 12.

26. Lucy Steinitz, "To End Apartheid," *New Menorah*, second series: no. 4, n.d., p. 5.

27. For an overview of Jewish feminism see Susannah Heschel, ed., *On Being a Jewish Feminist: A Reader* (New York: Schocken, 1983). From an Orthodox perspective see Blu Greenberg, *On Women and Judaism: A View from Tradition* (Philadelphia: The Jewish Publication Society of America, 1981).

28. Susan Weidman Schneider, *Jewish and Female: Choices and Changes in Our Lives Today* (New York: Simon and Schuster, 1985), pp. 5, 6.

29. Ibid., pp. 426–432.

30. Ibid., p. 95.

31. Ibid., p. 123.

32. "Evaluating a Decade of Jewish Feminism: An Inteview with Paula Hyman and Arlene Agus," *Lilith* (Fall/Winter 1983): 24. In the same vein Susannah Heschel writes, "The very bases of Judaism are being challenged—from *halakhah* to the prayer book to the very ways we conceive of God. The challenge emerging today demands a Copernican revolution: a new theology of Judaism, requiring new understanding of

God, revelation, *halakhah* and the Jewish people in order to support and encourage change." See Heschel, *Jewish Feminist*, p. xxiii.

CHAPTER 4

1. Michael Walzer, *Exodus and Revolution* (New York: Basic Books, 1985), p. 6.

2. James Cone, *Black Theology and Black Power* (New York: Seabury, 1969), pp. 6, 43, 44.

3. Ibid., p. 44.

4. Quoted by James Cone, *The Spirituals and the Blues* (New York: Seabury, 1972), p. 44.

5. Cone, *Black Theology*, pp. 39, 40. For Cone's later works see his *God of the Oppressed* (New York: Seabury, 1975) and *For My People: Black Theology of the Black Church* (Maryknoll, N.Y.: Orbis, 1984).

6. Second General Conference of Latin American Bishops, *The Church in the Present-Day Transformation of Latin America in Light of the Council* (Washington, D.C.: National Conference of Catholic Bishops, 1979), p. 28.

7. Gustavo Gutiérrez, *A Theology of Liberation: History, Politics and Salvation*, trans. Cardidad Inda and John Eagleson (Maryknoll, N.Y.: Orbis, 1973), pp. 155, 156.

8. Ibid., p. 157.

9. Ibid., p. 159.

10. Ibid., p. 177. Also see Gustavo Gutiérrez, *The Power of the Poor in History*, trans. Robert R. Barr (Maryknoll, N.Y.: Orbis, 1983). The use of the Exodus and of the prophets is not limited to American Blacks and Latin Americans. The African continent has been touched by theologies of liberation, most notably in South Africa. Starting in June 1985, as the most recent South African crisis was intensifying, a series of meetings of theologians and Church leaders took place in the heart of Soweto, its purpose to chart a course of action for Christians in the perilous waters of apartheid and the state of emergency. The meetings resulted in *The Kairos Document* published in September 1985, described by the authors as an "attempt by concerned Christians in South Africa to reflect on the situation of death in our country." Such reflection produced a critique of the current theological models used by the Church to resolve the problems of South Africa. Further, there was an attempt to develop an alternative biblical and theological model that would lead to forms of activity designed to affect the future. Not surprisingly, the authors found the Hebrew Scriptures to have much to say about their present situation, especially as seen through the Exodus experience. "The description of oppression in the Bible is concrete

and vivid. The Bible describes oppression as the experience of being crushed, degraded, humiliated, exploited, impoverished, defrauded, deceived and enslaved. And the oppressors are described as cruel, ruthless, arrogant, greedy, violent and tyrannical and as the enemy. Such descriptions could only have been written originally by people who had had a long and painful experience of what it means to be oppressed. And indeed nearly 90 percent of the history of the Jewish and later the Christian people whose story is told in the Bible, is a history of domestic or international oppression. Israel as a nation was built upon the painful experience of oppression and repression as slaves in Egypt. But what made all the difference for this particular group of oppressed people was the revelation of Yahweh. God revealed himself as Yahweh, the one who has compassion on those who suffer and who liberates them from their oppressors. 'I have seen the miserable state of my people in Egypt. I have heard their appeal to be free of their slave-drivers. I mean to deliver them out of the hands of the Egyptians. . . . The cry of the sons of Israel has come to me, and I have witnessed the way in which the Egyptians oppress them (Ex. 3: 7–9)' " (The Kairos Theologians, *The Kairos Document: Challenge to the Church* [Stony Point, New York: Theology Global Context, 1985], pp. i, 16).

11. Suh Kwang-Sun David, "A Biographical Sketch of an Asian Theological Consultation" in *Minjung Theology: People as the Subjects of History*, ed. Commission on Theological Concerns of the Christian Conference of Asia (Maryknoll, N.Y.: Orbis, 1983), p. 16.

12. Moon Hee-Suk Cyris, "An Old Testament Understanding of Minjung," in ibid., pp. 136, 137. For a more detailed discussion see Cyris, *A Korean Minjung Theology: An Old Testament Perspective* (Maryknoll, N.Y.: Orbis, 1986).

13. For a typical and unfortunately superficial response to Christian liberation theology see Leon Klenicki, "The Theology of Liberation: A Latin American Jewish Exploration," *American Jewish Archives* 35 (April 1983): 27–39.

14. This absence of a contemporary Jewish people is noticeable in all the liberation theologies cited above. Typical is Gutiérrez's discussion of the Exodus in his *A Theology of Liberation*, pp. 153–167.

15. For an example of an emphasis on the death of Jesus see Jon Sobrino, *Christology at the Crossroads: A Latin American Approach*, trans. John Drury (Maryknoll, N.Y.: Orbis, 1978). For an overall discussion of contemporary Christian and Jewish perspectives on the trial and death of Jesus see John T. Pawlikowski, "The Trial and Death of Jesus: Reflections in Light of a New Understanding of Judaism," *Chicago Studies* 25 (April 1986): 79–94.

16. Joan Casañas, "The Task of Making God Exist," in *The Idols of*

Death and the God of Life: A Theology, ed. Pablo Richard et al., trans. Barbara E. Campbell and Bonnie Shepard (Maryknoll, N.Y.: Orbis, 1983), p. 113.

17. Ibid., p. 114.

18. Ibid., p. 115.

19. Ibid., pp. 115, 116. He writes, "I do not believe that the Omipotent who, because he so chooses, shelves his omnipotence and allows himself to be oppressed and massacred with the people for the alleged reason that it is love that must conquer has proven to be the type of God whom the most altruistic and heroic activists experience as an ultimate dimension and horizon of their struggle" (p. 116).

20. Ibid., p. 121.

21. Ibid., pp. 133, 134.

22. For my own struggle with this question see Marc H. Ellis, "Toward a Contemporary Understanding of Exile," in *Israel, the Church and the World Religions Face the Future* (Tantur, Jerusalem: Ecumenical Institute for Theological Research Yearbook, 1983–1984), pp. 113–128.

23. In the District Court of Jerusalem, criminal case No. 40/61, the Attorney-General of the government of Israel v. Adolph Eichmann. Minutes of Session No. 30, pp. L1, M1, M2, N1.

24. Joyce Hollyday, "The Battle for Central America," *Sojourners* 11 (April 1982): 17.

25. Ernesto Cardenal, *The Gospel in Solentiname*, vol. 1, trans. Donald D. Walsh (Maryknoll, N.Y.: Orbis, 1982), pp. 255–256.

26. Quoted in Reuben Ainsztein, *Jewish Resistance in Nazi-Occupied Eastern Europe* (London: Paul Elek, 1974), pp. 643, 644.

27. Eyewitness account quoted in Eliezer Berkovits, *With God in Hell: Judaism in the Ghettos and Deathcamps* (New York: Sanhedrin Press, 1979), pp. 21, 22.

28. Quoted in Placido Erdozain, *Archbishop Romero: Martyr of Salvador*, trans. John McFadden and Ruth Warner (Maryknoll, N.Y.: Orbis, 1981), pp. 75–76.

29. Steven T. Katz defines the uniqueness of the Jewish Holocaust by distinguishing between two understandings of genocide. "The first form, (A), understands genocide as the intent to destroy the national, religious, or ethnic identity of a group. The second form, (B), understands genocide to be the intent to destroy physically all persons who identify with and are identified by a given national, religious, or ethnic identity." For Katz, the latter relates to the Jewish Holocaust and distinguishes it from all other mass death events. Katz concludes that the experience of the native American and Afro-American differs qualitatively from that of the Jewish Holocaust. But can these distinctions ultimately have any meaning, and do we not lose the blood of the innocent in these artificial categories? For

Katz's labored argument see his *Post-Holocaust Dialogues: Critical Studies in Modern Jewish Thought* (New York: New York University Press, 1985), pp. 286–317.

30. Jane Hunter, "Links to Guatemala: Doomed by Democracy?" *Israeli Foreign Affairs* 2 (January 1986): 1. The documentation that Hunter, herself a Jew, uses throughout her newsletter is overwhelmingly from Jewish sources in Israel published in Israeli newspapers and periodicals.

31. Jane Hunter, "Reagan's Unseen Ally in Central America: Israel Sends Arms to the Contras but Won't Show Its Face," *Israeli Foreign Affairs* 1 (December 1984): 1, 2.

32. Jane Hunter, "Israel and the Contras: A Bigger Role," *Israeli Foreign Affairs* 1 (May 1985): 1, 2. Also see Hunter, "South Africa, Israel, Supplying Contras," *Israeli Foreign Affairs* 2 (March 1986): 1,6.

33. Jane Hunter, "The Relationship Between Israel and South Africa: How Close?" *Israeli Foreign Affairs* 1 (February 1985), p. 1. For a more detailed analysis of this relationship see Hunter, *Undercutting Sanctions— Israel, the U.S. and South Africa* (Washington, D.C.: Washington Middle East Associates, 1986). Also see James Adams, *The Unnatural Alliance* (London: Quartet Books, 1984).

34. Ibid., p. 8.

35. Jane Hunter, "Tutu Abhors Holocaust Monopoly," *Israeli Foreign Affairs* 1 (September 1985), pp. 1, 6. For those Israelis who do realize the connection regarding fascism and suffering see Hunter, "Israel and South Africa: In the Present Tense, *Israeli Foreign Affairs* 2 (April 1986): 5, 6.

36. One of the reasons for supporting such foreign policy is the maintenance of a burgeoning military-industrial complex in Israel. Aaron Klieman, who teaches in the Political Science Department at Tel Aviv University, documents the Israeli arms industry in his book *Israel's Global Reach: Arms Sales as Diplomacy* (Washington: Pergamon-Brassey's, 1985).

37. Pablo Richard, "Biblical Theology of Confrontation with Idols," in *Idols of Death*, pp. 7, 9.

38. Ibid., p. 15.

39. Ibid., p. 19.

40. The contemporary Jewish understanding of idolatry issues from the Holocaust and is summarized by Emil Fackenheim: "In ancient times, the unthinkable Jewish sin was idolatry. Today it is to respond to Hitler by doing his work." Translated as the refusal to work for the survival of the Jewish people, this can issue into a new form of idolatry: survival for survival's sake. Greenberg adds a dialectical edge to Fackenheim by speaking of "burning children" and other attempts at genocide. We have seen, however, how difficult it is for Greenberg to remain consistent. Fack-

enheim and Greenberg move beyond most other contemporary Jewish understandings of idolatry that developed during the Cold War and emphasize the virtues of democracy over against the totalizing dimensions of state communism. My own sense is that the contribution of Christian understandings of idolatry to the Jewish community is that they force a political analysis and commitment and thus a discussion on how seemingly anti-idolatrous stances might in fact support injustice and become idolatry. See Fackenheim, *God's Presence in History: Jewish Affirmations and Philosophical Reflections* (New York: New York University, 1970), p. 81. Also see Will Herberg, *Judaism and Modern Man: An Interpretation of Jewish Religion* (Philadelphia: Jewish Publication Society of America, 1951) and Lawrence Troster, "No Other Gods Before Me," *Viewpoints* 13 (March 4, 1985): 5, 8.

CHAPTER 5

1. Hannah Arendt, *The Origins of Totalitarianism* (New York: Harcourt Brace, 1951). For my own understanding of this in a more extended form see Marc H. Ellis, *Faithfulness in an Age of Holocaust* (Amity, New York: Amity House, 1986).
2. Ellis, *Faithfulness*, pp. 59–61.
3. Ibid.
4. Walter Benjamin, "Theses on the Philosophy of History," in *Illuminations*, ed. Hannah Arendt, trans. Harry Zohn (New York: Schocken, 1978), p. 255.
5. Ibid.
6. Ibid., pp. 256, 257.
7. Ibid., p. 264.
8. Ellis, *Faithfulness*, pp. 54–56.
9. Etty Hillesum, *An Interrupted Life: The Diaries of Etty Hillesum 1941–43*, ed. J. G. Gaarlandt and trans. Jonathan Cape (New York: Pocket Books, 1985), p. ix.
10. Ibid., pp. x–xviii.
11. Ibid., pp. 194, 195.
12. Ibid., p. 255.
13. Ibid., pp. 186, 187.
14. Ibid., pp. 184, 185.
15. Hillesum was not alone in the use of prayer as a form of resistance. See Eliezer Berkovits, *With God in Hell: Judaism in the Ghettos and Death Camps* (New York: Sanhedrin Press, 1979). For the role of Jewish law during the Holocaust see Robert Kirschner, *Rabbinic Response of the Holocaust Era* (New York: Schocken, 1985) and Irving J. Rosenbaum, *The Holocaust and Halakhah* (New York: KTAV, 1976).

16. Hillesum, pp. 99–101.

17. Maurice Friedman, *Martin Buber's Life and Work: The Middle Years, 1923-1945* (New York: E. P. Dutton, 1983).

18. Martin Buber, "The Meaning of Zionism" in *A Land of Two Peoples: Martin Buber on Jews and Arabs*, ed. Paul R. Mendes-Flohr (New York: Oxford University Press, 1983), p. 181.

19. Ibid., pp. 182, 183.

20. Ibid., p. 183.

21. Ibid., pp. 183, 184.

22. Ibid., "Zionism and 'Zionism,' " p. 221.

23. Of course the critique of Israel from a Zionist perspective continues unabated. Recent examples include Bernard Avishai, *The Tragedy of Zionism: Revolution and Democracy in the Land of Israel* (New York: Farrar, Straus and Giroux, 1985); Amnon Rubinstein, *The Zionist Dream Revisited: From Herzl to Gush Emunim and Back* (New York: Schocken, 1984); Meron Benvenisti, *Conflicts and Contradictions* (New York: Villard, 1986).

24. Martin Buber, *I and Thou*, trans. Walter Kaufman (New York: Scribners, 1970), p. 168.

25. Martin Buber, *Eclipse of God* (New Jersey: Humanities Press, 1979), p. 129.

CHAPTER 6

1. Almost all Jewish theologians see the Six-Day War as the moment of consensus when the North American Jewish community viewed Israel as singularly important. Two factors were predominant in encouraging this view: the fear that if Israel lost the war another Holocaust was imminent; and a sense of pride that an empowered Jewish community, once dependent on the protection of others, could go it alone and win decisively. The other side of the war, though—increased militarization and the role of Israel as a conqueror—was not foreseen. This arrogance issued later into the need to assess the cost of empowerment. For two examples of the power of the 1967 war on Jewish theology see Emil Fackenheim, *God's Presence in History: Jewish Affirmations and Philosophical Reflections* (New York: New York University, 1970) and Irving Greenberg, "Cloud of Smoke, Pillar of Fire: Judaism, Christianity and Modernity After the Holocaust," in *Auschwitz: Beginning of a New Era?* ed. Eva Fleischner (New York: KTAV, 1977).

2. The challenge to the Jewish establishment occurred on at least two levels: the synagogue and Jewish organizations that did not have Israel as their primary focus. See Irving Greenberg's analysis of this situation in Chapter Two. The irony of the new consensus forged by the Holocaust

theologians who successfully challenged the old consensus is not lost on Roberta Strauss Feuerlicht; she writes that "dissidents are usually denied the opportunity to speak in synagogues or before Jewish groups." She correctly identifies the dilemma that follows: "To be able to criticize Israel without retribution one must be independent of the Jewish community, in which case 'Jewish credentials' are challenged." Feuerlicht thus agrees with Greenberg though from a different perspective: once theological disputations involved the possibility of censor; "Today criticism of Israel is grounds for excommunication from the Jewish community." See Feuerlicht, *The Fate of the Jews: A People Torn Between Israeli Power and Jewish Ethics* (New York: Times Books, 1983), pp. 281, 282.

3. As with any movement of dissent, the price to be paid is in the realm both of opportunity (speaking engagements and job possibilities, for example) and of psychology (the feeling of rejection and charges of traitorous activity, even consorting with the enemy). The most frequent accusation is that through dissent one is laying the groundwork for another Holocaust. The result is often self-censorship. Those who continue to speak realize that solidarity carries pain and sacrifice. Just as often, people of conscience drift away from identification with the Jewish community.

4. Perhaps this is the future of religious resistance: small groups within diverse communities who, while remaining rooted in their own community, come into solidarity with each other. See Chapter Four, "The Prophetic Voice in the Twentieth Century" in Marc H. Ellis, *Faithfulness in an Age of Holocaust* (Amity, New York: Amity House, 1986).

5. All the questions and assertions have been experienced by the author in travels in North America and around the world and even to some extent at Maryknoll. My point here is that it is difficult to be naive about anti-Semitism even among progressive Christians and humanists. However, should we be enslaved by anti-Semitism and live in fear and isolation? Or should we work toward a future where solidarity with all peoples, if not the norm, will at least surface in a dynamic and poignant way?

6. The constant equation of Yasser Arafat with Adolf Hitler in Jewish writing and public discussion exemplifies the exaggeration and denigration of the Palestinian people. Most of the world, as well as many officials within the United States government, sees Arafat as a moderate. See Alan Hart, *Arafat: Terrorist or Peacemaker* (London: Sidgwick and Jackson, 1984). To many, the restraint of the Palestinians enduring Israeli occupation has been remarkable. Alexander Cockburn writes that "according to B. Michael, writing in *Ha'aretz* in July 1982, 282 Israelis were killed by Palestinian violence between 1967 and 1982. During that time the rest of Palestine was occupied; 200,000 Palestinians expelled; Jerusalem annexed; thousands of Palestinian houses blown up on the West Bank and the Gaza Strip; and, according to Meron Benvenisti, approximately 52 percent of

Palestinian land in those areas expropriated." See Cockburn, "More Swill from Marty," *The Nation* 242 (March 15, 1986): 295.

7. See Rosemary Radford Ruether, *Faith and Fratricide: The Theological Roots of Anti-Semitism* (New York: Seabury, 1974) and Elisabeth Schüssler Fiorenza, *In Memory of Her: A Feminist Theological Reconstruction of Christian Origins* (New York: Crossroad, 1983); Isabel Carter Heyward, *The Redemption of God: A Theology of Mutual Redemption* (New York: University Press of America, 1982).

8. Attempts to heal the rift theologically often revolve around the person of Jesus. Two recent books by Jewish authors are interesting on this point. See Harvey Falk, *Jesus the Pharisee: A New Look at the Jewishness of Jesus* (New York: Paulist Press, 1985) and Pinchas Lapide, *The Sermon on the Mount: Utopia or Program for Action?* (Maryknoll, N.Y.: Orbis, 1986).

9. The Union of American Hebrew Congregations, the national coordinating organization for the Reform movement in North America, exemplifies the finest tradition of contemporary Jewish liberalism as well as its limitations. In their 58th General Assembly held in Los Angeles, October 31 to November 5, 1985, they approved, among others, resolutions on South Africa, sanctuary, AIDS and arms control. See Commission on Social Action of Reform Judaism, "Briefings," February 1986. Also see Albert Vorspan, *Great Jewish Debates and Dilemmas: Jewish Perspectives on Moral Issues in Conflict in the Eighties* (New York: Union of American Hebrew Congregations, 1980).

10. For the theme of affluence see Norman Podhoretz, *Making It* (New York: Harper and Row, 1980). For the social and political commitment of Jews without religious affiliation see the pages of the socialist periodical *Monthly Review.*

11. The problem is that while the Holocaust theologians quite correctly shifted the understanding of a practicing Jew to respond to the formative events of our time, the Holocaust and Israel took on religious connotations that many of the secular left could not accept. Another either/or situation was announced: either the Holocaust and Israel are the centers of your life, or you are not a practicing Jew. Jews on the secular left often see the Holocaust in relation to fascism and see Israel as a colonial imposition of the imperial west, so once again the division is present. My own sense is that a dialogue is needed if we are to move beyond the categories now in place, and that each side has a part of truth needed by the other. The Jewish community cannot move toward fidelity without the radical economic and political critique carried by the Jewish left, and the Jewish left cannot move beyond its own assumptions without the religious community. In effect this dialogue may be beginning through the curious paradox of the Jewish secular left's interest in Christian liberation theologies. While searching

for essays for a volume on Christian theologies of liberation, William Tabb, a secular Jewish leftist, was interested to hear of an emerging Jewish theology of liberation and decided to republish my first article on the subject. See William Tabb, ed., *Churches in Struggle: Liberation Theologies and Social Change in North America* (New York: Monthly Review Press, 1986), pp. 67-84.

12. The debate over the relationship between Israeli and Diaspora Jews is often emotional and angry. For the denigration of Diaspora Jews see A. B. Yehoshua, "Exile as a Neurotic Condition" in *Diaspora: Exile and the Jewish Condition*, ed. Etan Levine (New York: Jason Aronson, 1983), pp. 15-35. For the struggle of a Diaspora Jew to affirm the importance of diverse Jewish communities see Jacob Neusner, *Stranger at Home: The Holocaust, Zionism, and American Judaism* (Chicago: University of Chicago Press, 1981) and his *The Jewish War Against the Jews: Reflections on Golah, Shoah, and Torah* (New York: KTAV, 1984).

13. Feuerlicht correctly points out that 75 percent of the world's Jewish population does not live in Israel and that more than half a million Israelis have emigrated. Following David Ben Gurion, who said that only Jews planning to live in Israel should call themselves Zionists, Feuerlicht defines a non-Zionist as a Jew "who talks Zionism but lives in America." She concludes, "Zionism has always been a minority position among Jews and remains so; otherwise, there would not be so many Jews unwilling to settle in Israel." See Feuerlicht, *Fate of the Jews*, p. 220.

14. Interestingly, Emil Fackenheim insists that Christians must become Zionists in order to be authentic partners in dialogue. See his *To Mend the World: Foundations of Future Jewish Thought* (New York: Schocken Books, 1982), p. 303. Daniel Berrigan, however, a Jesuit priest who has spent a lifetime struggling against racism and militarism, committed the cardinal sin of speaking critically of Israel, and is thus shunned if not derided by many in the Jewish community. In general the Christian left, which has much to learn from and to offer the Jewish community, but in vision and commitment tends to be critical of Israeli policies, is automatically left out of the dialogue if Christian Zionism is the ticket of admission. A major thesis of this book is that it is precisely these groups that can journey with us to a future worth creating. Insisting on Christian Zionism will increasingly leave us with alliances that portend betrayal. Do these powerful Christians who often celebrate Israel for its Western orientation and effective military really have our interests at heart?

AFTERWORD

1. Michael Lerner, "The Occupation: Immoral and Stupid," *Tikkun* 3 (March/April 1988): 8. Lerner continues: "The crisis in Israel is a moment

of truth for all of us. It should be responded to with the deepest seriousness and with the full understanding that the choices we make now may have consequences that reverberate for centuries to come" (p. 12).

2. Johann Baptist Metz, *The Emergent Church: The Future of Christianity in a Postbourgeois World*, trans. Peter Mann (New York: Crossroad, 1981), p. 19. This is *not* an attempt to compare the Nazi period with the Israeli-Palestinian conflict or to create a scenario of evil Israelis and innocent Palestinians. Neither do I want to suggest that Palestinians have only been victimized by Israelis. It is to suggest that Israel, at this point in history, is powerful and thus the responsibility is clear. Further, it is to suggest that even justice is not enough. We can only move forward *with* the Palestinian people.

3. For a discussion of dissent and Israel's nuclear capability see Rudolf Peierls, "The Case of Mordechai Vanunu," *New York Review of Books* 35 (June 16, 1988): 56. Also see Jane Hunter, "Vanunu and Israel's Nuclear Crimes," *Israeli Foreign Affairs* 4 (February 1988): 3. For the fate of the young during the uprising see *Palestinians Killed by Israeli Occupation Forces, Settlers, and Civilians During Uprising, December 9, 1987, through April 18, 1988*, (Chicago: Database Project on Palestinian Human Rights, 1988), and *Children of the Stones,* (Jerusalem: Palestinian Center for the Study of Nonviolence, 1988). For the response of Irving Greenberg to the uprising see his "The Ethics of Jewish Power," *Perspectives* (New York: National Jewish Center for Learning and Leadership, 1988). For the response of Elie Wiesel see his "A Mideast Peace - Is it Impossible?" *New York Times,* June 23, 1988, p. 22.

4. A major task of theology is to nurture the questions a people need to ask about the future they are creating. In its time Holocaust theology did this and thus reoriented most of Jewish theology and Jewish secular thought. But today Holocaust theology is distant from the history we are creating and therefore applies past categories to present realities. Our behavior is filtered through this framework: that which cannot happen within this framework thus by definition is not happening. Two options appear. Either we lose touch with the history we are creating, producing dissonance, a sense of isolation, paralysis, or even cynicism; or if we understand the history we are creating, we do so uncritically. Hence the neoconservative drift in Jewish theology. When theology ceases to nurture the questions a people need to ask about the history they are creating, critical thought atrophies. In the case of the Jewish people more than thought is at stake: We are in danger of becoming everything we loathed about our oppressors.

5. For an important historical understanding of the interaction of Israel and Palestine see Simha Flapan, *The Birth of Israel: Myths and Realities* (New York: Pantheon, 1987). Flapan, a life-long Zionist and

resident of Israel/Palestine from 1930 until his death in 1987, writes that Israel's myths, "forged during the formation of the state have hardened into this impenetrable, and dangerous, ideological shield" (p. 8). To understand the contemporary scene, Flapan reassesses the birth of Israel and in a sense his own birth as a Zionist. On the subject of the Israel-South Africa relationship after its announced termination in 1987, see Jane Hunter, "South Africa Hurls Israeli Technology Against Angola, May Build Lavi Aircraft," *Israeli Foreign Affairs* 3 (December 1987): 1,5, and ibid., "Israelis Help South African Air Force," *Israeli Foreign Affairs* 4 (April 1988): 1,8.

6. One such attempt to break through the silence is found in David Grossman's *The Yellow Wind,* trans. Haim Watzman (New York: Farrar, Straus and Giroux, 1988). In the wake of the uprising it became a bestseller in Israel and the United States.

7. For the first publication of the Committee Confronting the Iron Fist, see *We Will Be Free in Our Own Homeland: A Collection of Readings for International Day of Fast and Solidarity with Palestinian Prisoners,* (Jerusalem, 1986). A report on *Yesh Gvul* can be found in "Israeli Doves Arousing Little Response," *New York Times,* March 1, 1988. See also "A Captain's Ideals Lead Him to Jail," ibid., March 20, 1988 and Gideon Spiro, "The Israeli Soldiers Who Say 'There is a Limit,' " *Middle East International* No. 333 (September 9, 1988): 18-20.

8. For New Jewish Agenda's response to the uprising see Ezra Goldstein and Deena Hurwitz, "No Status Quo Ante" *New Jewish Agenda* 24 (Spring 1988): 1-3. Arthur Hertzberg is probably the most articulate and widely read Jewish intellectual on the uprising. See his "The Uprising" *New York Review of Books* 35 (February 4, 1988): 30-32, and "The Illusion of Jewish Unity," *New York Review of Books,* 35 (June 16, 1988): 6, 8, 10–12. Also see the cable sent to the President of Israel by Rabbi Alexander M. Schindler, President of the Union of American Hebrew Congregations, found in *AS Briefings: Commission on Social Action of Reform Judaism,* March, 1988, Appendix A. He begins the cable, "I am deeply troubled and pained in sending you this message, but I cannot be silent. The indiscriminate beating of Arabs, enunciated and implemented as Israel's new policy to quell the riots in Judea, Samaria and Gaza, is an offense to the Jewish spirit. It violates every principle of human decency. And it betrays the Zionist dream." Also see Albert Vorspan, "Soul Searching," *New York Times Magazine,* May 8, 1988, pp. 40–41, 51, 54.

9. Shamir's response is a prime lesson in Holocaust theology. At a news conference in Jerusalem, Shamir said: "It is the height of temerity and hypocrisy that members of the terrorist organization speak of returning. This boat which loads its decks with murderers, terrorists who sought to

murder us—all of us, each of us. They wish to bring them to the land of Israel, and demonstrate that they are returning to the same place in which they wished to slay us. We will and do view this as a hostile act, an act which endangers the state of Israel." Quoted in "Israel's Furious Over a Palestinian Plan to 'Return' to Haifa by Sail," *New York Times,* February 11, 1988, p. 15.

10. See Rosemary Radford Ruether and Herman J. Ruether, *The Wrath of Jonah: The Crisis of Religious Nationalism in the Israeli-Palestinian Conflict* (San Francisco: Harper and Row, 1988). For a fascinating Jewish response to Christian critical solidarity with the Jewish people see *Interreligious Currents,* ed. Annette Daum, 7 (Winter/Spring 1988): 1-8.

11. The strains of this highly problematic and emotional relationship have increasingly come to the surface in recent years. Witness the upheavals in North American Jewish life relating to the Lebanese War, the massacres at Sabra and Shatila, the Pollard spy case, and now the uprising. My point is simply that the relationship between Jews in Israel and Jews outside of Israel cannot remain as it is without ultimately dividing the community at its very roots.

12. For Hannah Arendt's prophetic understanding of the choices facing the Jewish settlers in Palestine, see a collection of her essays *Hannah Arendt; the Jew as Pariah: Jewish Identity and Politics in the Modern Age,* ed. Ron H. Feldman (New York: Grove Press, 1978).

Suggested Readings

Avishai, Bernard. *The Tragedy of Zionism: Revolution and Democracy in the Land of Israel.* New York: Farrar Straus Giroux, 1985.

Benvenisti, Meron. *Conflicts and Contradictions.* New York: Villard Books, 1986.

Buber, Martin. *A Land of Two Peoples: Martin Buber on Jews and Arabs.* Edited by Paul Mendes-Flohr. New York: Oxford University Press, 1983.

Fackenheim, Emil. *God's Presence in History: Jewish Affirmations and Philosophical Reflections.* New York: New York University Press, 1970.

———. *To Mend the World: Foundations of Future Jewish Thought.* New York: Schocken, 1982.

Feuerlicht, Roberta Strauss. *The Fate of the Jews: A People Torn Between Israeli Power and Jewish Ethics.* New York: Times Books, 1983.

Findley, Paul. *They Dare to Speak Out: People and Institutions Confront Israel's Lobby.* Westport, Connecticut: Laurence Hill, 1985.

Fleischner, Eva, ed. *Auschwitz: Beginning of a New Era? Reflections on the Holocaust.* New York: KTAV, 1977.

Greenberg, Blu. *On Women and Judaism: A View from Tradition.* Philadelphia: Jewish Publication Society of America, 1981.

Greenberg, Irving. "On the Third Era on Jewish History: Power and Politics" in *Perspectives.* New York: National Jewish Resource Center, 1980.

———. "The Third Great Cycle in Jewish History" in *Perspectives.* New York: National Jewish Resource Center, 1981.

Heschel, Susannah, ed. *On Being a Jewish Feminist: A Reader.* New York: Schocken Books, 1983.

Hilberg, Raul. *The Destruction of the European Jews.* New York: Harper and Row, 1961.

Hillesum, Etty. *An Interrupted Life: The Diaries of Etty Hillesum 1941–43.* New York: Pocket Books, 1985.

Hunter, Jane. *Undercutting Sanctions: Israel, the U.S. and South Africa.* Washington, D.C.: Washington Middle East Associates, 1986.

Klieman, Aaron S., *Israel's Global Reach: Arms Sales as Diplomacy.* Washington: Pergamon-Brassey's, 1985.

Morley, John F. *Vatican Diplomacy and the Jews During the Holocaust 1939–1943.* New York: KTAV, 1980.

Oz, Amos. *In the Land of Israel.* New York: Harcourt Brace Jovanovich, 1983.

Reisman, Bernard. *The Chavurah: A Contemporary Jewish Experience.* New York: Union of American Hebrew Congregations, 1977.

Rubenstein, Richard. *After Auschwitz: Radical Theology and Contemporary Judaism.* New York: Bobbs-Merrill, 1966.

———. *The Cunning of History: Mass Death and the American Future.* New York: Harper and Row, 1975.

Schiff, Ze'ev and Enud Ya'ari. *Israel's Lebanon War.* New York: Simon and Schuster, 1984.

Schneider, Susan Weidman. *Jewish and Female: Choices and Changes in Our Lives Today.* New York: Simon and Schuster, 1985.

Shorris, Earl. *Jews Without Mercy: A Lament.* Garden City, New York: Doubleday, 1982.

Walzer, Michael. *Exodus and Revolution.* New York: Basic Books, 1985.

Waskow, Arthur. *Godwrestling.* New York: Schocken Books, 1978.

———. *These Holy Sparks: The Rebirth of the Jewish People.* New York: Harper and Row, 1983.

Wiesel, Elie. *Night.* New York: Avon, 1969.

———. *A Jew Today.* New York: Random House, 1978.

Wyman, David S. *The Abandonment of the Jews: America and the Holocaust 1941–1945.* New York: Pantheon, 1984.

Index

Compiled by William E. Jerman